The Making of Santa

By

James Brown

Tinsel Thyme Press

Published by: Tinsel Thyme Press, LLC, Warrenton, VA, email: tinselthymepress@gmail.com

ISBN: 978-1-7347906-0-3
Library of Congress Control Number: 2022907927
Printed in the United States of America

ACKNOWLEDGMENTS

I have been overwhelmed by the interest, support, and assistance offered by so many colleagues, family members, and friends during my work on this book and I have no words of gratitude that could ever say enough. I would like to thank my team of editors that have struggled through this book with me – Deborah McLean and Katherine Eppley – your help has been invaluable by doing the impossible with my writing and finally, to my bride Nichole – your support has been true and beautiful, thank you. To my biggest supporter, Zechariah Brown, your help and comments were invaluable during this process. There have been so many others that have helped me while writing this book – Phillip Wenz, Dutch Schrap, Thomas Sheerin, Kathleen Healy, Reverend Dr. Dennis R. Di Mauro, Travis Rogers, Sherrie Davidson, Timothy MacQuarrie, Susan Oltz, Gary Patishnock, Brandi Zahir, and Justin Pregenzer.

Table of Contents

"Whatever you do, do it well. Do it so well that when people see you do it they will want to come back and see you do it again and they will want to bring others and show them how well you do what you."
— Walt Disney

Being Santa is not easy!!!

You have made the biggest decision of your life – you want to be Santa Claus. Your life will never be the same. Moms, Dads, and children will search you out to come by so you can spread some Christmas magic. It's not easy being Santa – I will not lie to you. But I will be honest with you – I would not give this up for anything in the world – it is worth the effort!!!

With that said, "Congratulations." You have made the biggest investment in your Santa career by purchasing this book, which I hope that you will use to your full advantage. This book is unlike many of the training manuals currently out in the Santa Community provided by several current Santa schools and classes. This book provides you with the blueprints to get your Santa portrayal up and running.

I believe that to be a first-rate Christmas performer, there are three basic concepts– do historical research of your character; rehearse your role by incorporating your research; and finally, fully developing your portrayal of your character Santa. As with any occupation, first you need to research and understand the historical aspect of your Christmas character. I have thoroughly researched the rumors and ran them to conclusion. To this end, I have researched and confirmed historical documents including Santa Community documents, magazines, newspapers, interviews, and personal interviews, thus having essential primary and secondary resources. Within this book I have provided my own research so you can dig deeper and expand upon it for your Christmas performer experience.

The second basic concept is to rehearse and immerse yourself into your character. The old saying is "rehearse, rehearse, rehearse." Take the historical information that you have learned and build it into your character. Know your background story well enough that you are prepared to answer questions from your audience regarding your Santa persona.

The third basic concept is to develop your portrayal of your character. It's showtime! This is the moment that you take everything you have learned about your character and incorporated into your role. Then, having worked out all the glitches, you are ready to make your grand performance to the public.

It's up to you to measure how successful you are in the public light. Keep a journal of your performances. Keep track of everthing. Be humble if something does not work well and be proud of what does work well. Adjust your character as you move forward, to address what is not working, as well as striving to improve each performance.

In this book, I discuss how to set up your Santa business for you to operate in the years to come. My goal is to provide you the tools to operate confidently as your character develops. I purposely wrote the book to examine the various elements of running a business and tried to cover as much as possible in generic terms. I intentionally left detailed technology information out of the book since it changes every five minutes. This book was designed to stand the test of time. As they say, today's technology will be gone tomorrow.

I wrote this book on the preface not to endorse any Santa schools, Santa businesses or Santa organizations outright. It is my belief that each individual Santa or Mrs. Claus should make his/her decision about the services offered to the Santa community. Each Santa or Mrs. Claus needs to to develop their own character to fit their personal portrayal – not to be flooded with advertisements.

Therefore, I chose not to include any current named Santa business or Santa schools. In today's Santa community there is a plethora of Santa schools and businesses listed on any Santa Facebook site. As for Santa organizations, there is a current list, but as the author of this book, I will not endorse anyone for the record.

I decided while researching this book that I came across too much information to put into one single book. So, I opted to create a second book to discuss the historical aspects of the Santa Community which will help with your character portrayal. The second book will contain the roots of the magic and mystery of the origins of the Santa legend.

I look forward to helping you with your Santa Business, so let's start the journey together!

James Brown

Chapter 1

Setting Up Your Business

"Christmas is the season for kindling the fire of hospitality in the hall, the genial flame of charity in the heart."
— Washington Irvin

Setting Up Your Business

Now since you are here looking to learn more about the business of being Santa, you need to clearly understand a basic fact of life... Running a Santa business is a very niche business. What does that mean? Well, it means you are not going to get rich overnight, no matter what you have heard or read.

For the majority of Santas, the normal business cycle is seven weeks each year in which to generate most of our income. Some of the big box stores start having Santa in their stores as soon as Veterans Day weekend until Christmas Eve, which is normally from the weekend of 11th November until 24th December.

In the Santa community, there is no one business model that fits every Santa. Your Santa portrayal is unique to your own strengths and weakness. This is a business where you set your own standard. You set your own budget, your own prices, pay your own taxes, hire your own staff, and figure out what services you will provide.

The next section will provide information to help make an educated decision on how to run your business. You will be cautioned that any decision you make is yours and yours alone. It is certainly recommended that you take this information and check with a qualified certified public accountant (CPA), financial advisor, or local tax attorney, and/or your local government office to understand the rules, regulations, taxes/fees and laws in your area for small businesses.

Spend time to understand a traditional business model which includes developing your Executive Summary which contains a mission statement that helps describe who and why you are being Santa. Secondly, when using the business model, you need to consider your business structure (aka legal requirements such as registering your business with the local government). Thirdly, the next item would be the marketing structure of your business. This includes how to generate a plan to promote, advertise and price your services and products. Lastly, you need to consider what your financials for the business is going to look like.

Tips that Businesses and Organizations Look for in a Santa

In 2011, Thumbtack published the article, "Santa's business: An in-depth look at the thriving Santa industry", which shared several points about your reputation as Santa. Based upon personal experience, be aware that families will attend a public function in order to check how a particular Santa interacts with the children and parents before booking a session with that Santa.

Here are some of the top consumer tips listed in the article:

Safety – Santas must ensure SAFETY as a top priority. Most Santas will provide the results of an annual background check which provide the parents a sense of security when you are dealing with their children. Another item to consider is obtaining liability insurance and then being able to inform your client that you carry liability insurance.

Experience – Something to consider is the number of years you have been portraying Santa. How do you handle the most awkward situations/questions such as: Can you help mommy and daddy get back together again? Inexperienced Santas need to learn from the experienced Santas how to handle the most delicate scenarios.

Personality – When it comes to picking a Santa, you can't just go by what you read. You've got to call up your potential St. Nick and chat for a while in order to get a genuine sense of how he interacts with people. The best Santas genuinely love meeting people. They understand how to listen and interact with children, and they are pros at conveying a sense of magic and excitement.

Differences Between a
Sole Proprietorship & Limited Liability Company (LLC)

Making the decision to take the Santa business from a hobby to a business is a big step. One of the biggest decisions that you will have at the onset involves determining your business structure. This discussion is limited in scope and focus to an LLC and Sole Proprietorship since only Santa businesses are discussed. There are several differences between these two business structures. An LLC provides the same protection as a corporation and the operational flexibility of a partnership. On the other hand, sole proprietorships are the easiest and most cost-effective type of business to form and operate.

Differences in Liability Protection
One of the biggest differences between a sole proprietorship and an LLC is the issue of limited liability protection. In the Santa business, most Santas do carry the industry standard insurance policy which will protect from a lawsuit. However, in the event a lawsuit exceeds those limits, the business may end up becoming a liability. Some examples of this situation are shown below.

Sole proprietors are personally responsible for all business debts, lawsuits and other business-related obligations. Basically, if the business cannot meet the company's debts, creditors may go after a sole proprietor's personal assets to satisfy the obligation.

Running your Santa business as an LLC provides you as the owner protection against company debts and obligations, in case you default. Creditors and parties who initiate a lawsuit against an LLC cannot go after an owner's personal assets as compensation for business-related debts.

Differences in Owner Control

The sole proprietor alone will have to make every decision regarding how to operate the company and use the company's resources. Other people are not responsible for bad ideas. To emphasize this point: Only the sole proprietor is responsible for any decisions regarding his own Santa business.

LLCs with more than one owner will have other members and managers to provide input regarding how to manage the business. Thus, the responsibility for all decisions within the LLC is shared.

Ease of Raising Money

In the Santa business, most will only invest the money available on hand - in essence a cash business. However, if you decide to borrow money, just remember that statistically, sole proprietorships have more difficulty raising money than an LLC.

Number of Owners

A business can have only one person acting as the company's owner in order to be a sole proprietorship. Conversely, an LLC may have an unlimited number of owners that may consist of foreign businesses, corporations, other LLCs and partnerships, if you have an operating agreement.

Existence and Lifespan

An LLC may exist forever, regardless of who the manager or members of the company are. LLCs may have an operating agreement that indicates provisions for continuing the company in the event of a member's death, withdrawal or retirement. A sole proprietorship will cease to exist when a business owner dies, retires or decides to sell the business.

	Limited Liability Company (LLC)	Sole Proprietorship
Meaning	Decisions are made by the members of the company.	Decisions are made by the sole owner of the company.
Separate Entity	An LLC and its members are separate entities.	The company and the owner do not have any separate legal entity.
Forming Formalities	To form an LLC, the member(s) need to register as per state regulations.	The owners need to ensure that he/she is not using a business name that is already established.
Fees for Forming	To file, the cost can range up to $1,000 depending on the state.	No cost to form the business in most states.
Taxation	Single method of taxing: Taxes are charged at members' rates.	Taxes are charged on the income of the owner.
Liability Protection	For an LLC, the members are liable to the extent of the investments into the LLC.	The owner is responsible for the entire operation. There is no liability protection.
Paperwork	Formal paperwork needs to be filed with the State Corporation Commission in order to create the business.	There is no formal paperwork to file to create the business.

Registering Your Santa Business

1. Register Your Business with the State Corporation Commission

Use a catchy name for your Santa business such as a regional name, local name, or your name like "Santa Bob". Your Santa business name needs to be unique and something no other Santa business currently uses. Check with your State Corporation Commission (SCC) to see if that name will be valid in your state. Do this first, before anything else! Search URLs to find out if your desired name is available on Facebook or the internet. Then check the internet to see if you can purchase the web domain for that name. Before registering your name, check everywhere you can possibly can look on the internet and with government/business links. Your business name becomes a "legal business name" in your state and also becomes your advertising tool.

2. Get Your Employer Identification Number

After registering your business name, go to the IRS homepage and get a Federal Employer Identification Number (EIN) - **https://www.irs.gov/businesses/small-businesses-self-employed/apply-for-an-employer-identification-number-ein-online**. This number will be used with the State Tax office, business banking accounts, and collecting payments from businesses. Using an EIN reduces the chances of identity theft associated with your social security number. It's free and only takes a couple of minutes to do the paperwork online.

3. Register Your Trade Name

Once you have completed the paperwork online for registering your business, your locality may require you to register a trade name (different from your business name). You will need to check with your county courthouse. This is usually a ten-minute process to fill out the paperwork and pay the fees. You should be able to be approved on the spot. You can do business under a different name than your company name. (A "doing business as" or "dba" form takes minutes to complete.)

Note: After completing these steps, ask your local government for guidance on how to finish your business process since Steps 4 through 10 will be based upon your locality. Always check with local officials.

4. Get a Zoning Permit for Your Business

Remember, Santa needs an office and storage area for his suits and record keeping documents. In some localities, having a home office will require a small business license. This can take up to a week or more to authorize a "home business occupation permit." This document is the basis for a home office tax deduction for your business.

5. Get Your Business License

After getting your Zoning Permit for your business license, apply for a business license. The form takes minutes to fill out. Use your EIN instead of your Social Security number to identify your business (for privacy reasons, if nothing else). A business license will allow you to purchase your items for business at wholesale prices.

6. Complete a Business Personal-Property Tax Form (if necessary)

Businesses are taxed on "personal" property, just like individuals. Check to see if a business property tax form is required for the year the business is established, but then required every year afterwards, or if it is required from the onset of your Santa business.

7. Contact Your State Department of Taxation

By contacting your state's office of taxation and registering with the taxation office, you are allowed to collect state sales tax on any products sold. (In most states, there is no sales tax on services). Also, you can apply for a "Certificate of Resale" which could make your purchases for the business sales tax-free. Check with your state to find out the rules.

8. Get a Business Checking/Savings Account

One of the easiest ways to make or receive payments and pay bills for your business is to establish a checking account specifically for your Santa business. The next section includes more details on why this is important.

9. Set up a Simple Accounting Spreadsheet

One of the easiest ways to ruin your business is by not having a method to track of your expenses, income, and mileage. The method of recording your information is dependent on what you and your Certified Public Accountant (CPA) decide is best for you.

10. Social Media Presence

As with any business, once you start the process to become established, it is important that you own the social media sites with your business name. Ensure that you can get the websites and Facebook sites with your desired name. As stated earlier, this should be one of the very first things you do as you set up your business. Please check out the Social Media section for more information.

Banking

Once you have established your Santa business as a true business, most CPAs would recommend that you open a bank account such as a checking account just for your business.

There are four excellent reasons to consider this:

1. This separates your business income from your personal income in case you are ever sued for any reason.

2. A business checking/savings account provides a buffer between your personal and business funds, which prevents personal funds being consumed by the business by mistake.

3. This account will protect your personal finances in case there is an Internal Revenue Service (IRS) or State Audit on your business.

4. A business account will allow you to obtain a business credit card to make your purchases. Having a business account also provides creditability with other businesses.

Most credit unions/banks require the following documents to open a business account, so be sure to bring them with you to open the new account:

— Certificate of Organization from the State Business Commission
— Partnership Agreement
— Business Organization Documents
— IRS EIN Letter
— Fictious Name Document
— Business Occupation Permit
— Business License

Taxes

Every year in January, the question pops up on social media sites: What is taxable, non-taxable, or deductible? First, contact a Certified Public Accountant (CPA), bookkeeper, or a professional tax preparer for advice. Please understand that blogs and what is said on social media do not always pertain to your specific situation. It is recommended that you take the time and sit down to discuss your *"financial state"* with someone who is knowledgeable on the current laws regarding taxes before the end of the tax year.

A CPA is required to tell you what the law is regarding your tax situation. If he/she gave you incorrect advice, he/she will be "on the hook" for that information and your tax return.

Another quick way to figure what the IRS is considering for your business: Go to the IRS website and check out the Schedule C form (**https://www.irs.gov/pub/irs-pdf/f1040sc.pdf**). One of the defining questions as to whether you can use the business deduction for Santa is "Have you invested 500 hours in your Santa business for this tax season?"

Personal Note: In my portrayal of Santa, I run Santa as a business through the Commonwealth of Virginia as an LLC to maximize the protection afforded under the law and to maximize the tax benefits. In doing so, I use business software such as QuickBooks, which I received free from the state for small businesses.[2] I downloaded the program and sat down with my Certified Public Accountant (CPA) to make a list of items which needed to be tracked for tax purposes.

CPAs will often defer to the Audit Techniques Guide (ATG) which provides technical information for common issues usually addressed during the tax season and the items on which an auditor will focus. A good CPA will use this guide to assist you in guiding you for your particular tax situation. In theory, Santas fall under the Entertainment Audit Technique Guide. The guide contains examination techniques, common and unique industry issues, business practices, industry terminology and other information to assist examiners in performing audit examinations.[3] You can find this guide at **https://www.irs.gov/pub/irs-utl/entertainmentatg.pdf**.

A suggested rule of thumb: If it cannot be used for other purposes and is purchased specifically and exclusively for your Santa business, it is usually deductible.

Always keep receipts your receipts for seven years. Scan all your hard copy receipts onto an external storage device in addition to placing them in an envelope. The traditional receipts printed on the wax paper usually disappears within 18 months.

By establishing Santa as a business with a dedicated bank account, you can more easily track your expenses with a dedicated bank card. You just never know when you could be audited for your business. In addition, as a registered business you could use a tax-exempt status on our purchases.

Example Item	Explanations
Santa suit	Yes, since it's used only for Santa portrayal clothing.
Santa belt	Yes, if used only for Santa portrayal clothing.
Santa eyewear	IF only used for Santa portrayal, then Yes. IF worn for personal use, then NO since this is a personal medical expense.
Traditional Santa beard/wig set	Yes, if used only for Santa portrayal.
Santa chair	Yes, IF decorative only and not used outside of Santa events.
Candy canes, trading cards, pens, pencils, toys, etc.	Yes, if exclusively purchased and used for Santa business.
Memberships to Santa organizations	Yes
Classes, symposiums, meetings, workshops and/or fees or dues	Yes
Santa Liability Insurance	Yes
Santa Business License	Yes
Santa Annual Background Check	Yes
Santa Ads, Signs, business cards, and vehicle signs	Yes
Santa Busines Property Taxes	Yes
Lease for Office Space	Yes, only a dedicated space for Santa
Books for your Santa business	Yes, only for Santa business

Trickler Item	Explanations
Software, computer equipment, cameras, electronics & related items	Probably yes, IF it is only used for the Santa business. You must prove the equipment is dedicated and cannot be used in everyday life. Check with your tax advisor.
Storage containers	Yes, if used only for Santa business items.
Hair care products	This gets complicated. If you bleach year-round, it may not be deductible; unless it's for Santa events. If you use styling tools and products year-round, it may not be deductible. Check with your tax advisor!
Home phone or cell phone	You can usually deduct a portion. Check with your tax advisor.
Internet	You can usually deduct a portion. Check with your tax advisor.
Santa chair	Yes, if exclusively purchased and used for Santa business.
Boots	Do you wear them to ride your motorcycle? No. If worn only for Santa events, then yes.
Website and Domain name	Only for Santa Business.
Home office	Check locality rules and check with your tax advisor.
Mileage	A qualified yes. Speak with your tax advisor, keep good records. It can get a little complicated - donated time as a volunteer, for example can count as a donation. Get advice from your tax advisor. KEEP GOOD RECORDS.

ALWAYS, ALWAYS, ALWAYS, talk to your tax advisor.

Background Checks

Every year thousands of Santas hit the street looking for work at charitable organizations, chain retail stores, shopping malls, individual retail stores, and local municipalities. In 2010, it was estimated that 7% of the Santas that were hired were ineligible for employment to due crimes involving some form of sexual misconduct which includes indecent exposure; assault; drunken driving; soliciting prostitution; and contributing to the delinquency of a minor.[5]

In today's society, a background check is a requirement to in order to receive Abuse and Molest coverage which is offered by most performer insurance companies. Always use a third-party vendor for the background check. If in doubt as to how or where to obtain a background check, please remember that Federal/State/Local Law Enforcement Agencies do background checks for a fee.

Listing yourself as a "background checked Santa" provides a sense of security for the parents and events coordinators before they pick-up the phone to call you. Having this displayed prominently in your business marketing allows parents and event coordinators to know you have gone "the extra mile" to increase safety for the children. This could mean more job opportunities for your business.

As part of your marketing promotion listing yourself as a "background checked Santa" provides a sense of security for the parents and events coordinators before they pick-up the phone to call you.

Social Media Background Checks

As a Christmas performer, we have all had some type of a background check for working with children. However, you may have never heard of a "Social Background Check." A social media background check is when an employer reviews a candidate's social media profiles to see whether he or she will be a good representative of their company. In other words, if you are hired for an event, will your past behavior be revealed and cause an embarrassment to the organization?

Note: Before you start advertising for Santa job opportunities, take the time to review all your social media accounts and remove any pictures and posts which might detract from hiring you.

Background checks are usually done towards the end of the hiring process and can reveal information not found in traditional screenings. With the intention of shielding companies from lawsuits and provide impartial information, background checks are hired out to a third-party company. According to the survey conducted by The Harris Poll on behalf of CareerBuilder, 47% percent of the hiring managers said that if they can't find a job candidate online, they are less likely to call that person in for an interview. Every Santa should have a professional business Facebook page, not connected to his personal social media.

According to the Federal Trade Commission, the prospective company is required to inform you in writing that a background check will be done, and you must provide permission for this to take place. In addition, an employer is required to provide you a copy of the report in case you may want to dispute the information. (See 15 U.S.C. section 168d (a), (b)).

Creating a Social Media presence will be discussed later in this book.

In 2018, Career Builder listed the criteria that businesses used to refrain from hiring individuals. [6] That criterion includes the following:

Crime — Posts (and these include memes, photos, cartoons, articles from legitimate sources) that may indicate the candidate was involved in a crime or supports crimes committed by another person or persons.[7]

Violence — Posts that may support or incite violence.

Prejudice — Posts that may contain racism, sexism, homophobia, racial slurs, stereotypes, or other forms of intolerance and hate speech.

Sexism — Posts that may indicate prejudice, stereotyping, or discrimination based on sex or gender.

Illicit Drugs or Substances — Posts that may promote illegal drugs or the practice of using illegal drugs/abusing prescriptions.

Provided false information — Either about qualifications or taking time off from work.

Posts were deemed inappropriate — Either provocative or inappropriate photographs, videos or bad mouth previous employer or employees.

On the other hand, companies listed favorable reasons why they hired a candidate. Social media accounts which contained the following were considered favorable:

Conveyed a **professional image and creativity** along with awards and accolades.

Supported their **professional qualifications** for the job and showed a well-rounded, showed a wide range of interests.

Showed the job **candidate's personality,** could see a good fit within the company culture.

Positive interaction with the hiring company's social media accounts.

Could positively **influence** a large number of individuals.

Liability Insurance

Personal Note: During my first couple of years of playing Santa, I did not carry liability insurance as Santa Claus. As I progressed through the ranks of becoming a traditional-bearded Santa, the need for insurance became important. The number of families that I started to visit increased, which led to businesses hearing about the great reviews Santa was receiving and Santa was soon popping up everywhere for events.

In the business world, to entice customers in, you must promote an item that the customers want. My first paid business event was at the regional hotel event called "Breakfast with Santa." In order to protect the business from anything I did, the hotel management required me to carry a liability policy. Less liabilities for them means a bigger profit margin for them. As my favorite financial gurus have said, ***"The primary purpose of insurance is to transfer the risk of financial loss from you to the insurance company."*** [8]

Santa Claus liability insurance helps keep the holidays jolly and worry-free of Grinch-like lawsuits. Whether you work full-time, part-time, seasonal, or as a volunteer at a shopping mall, store, parades, tree lightings, holiday parties or charity events, you should protect yourself from the uncertainties of the business by acquiring liability insurance. The majority of all businesses that hire Santa will require some type of insurance policy.

Santa liability insurance policy is designed to help you if a child falls off your lap, trips over your boots, chokes on a candy cane or cookie, or just slips and falls near you. Molestation insurance will cover you in case of allegations of misconduct or inappropriate touching which could result in another lawsuit and be the end of your Santa career. This could also result in other dire consequences. (Most group insurance policies will require a background check before covering you.)

According to "The International Council of Shopping Centers" study, Santa continues draw big crowds at shopping malls. As much as half of adults visiting a shopping center with children under the age of 13 plan to have their child's picture taken with Santa during the holiday season.[9] A mall Santa will typically see over 10,000 children in the six-week work period between Thanksgiving and Christmas.[10] Those numbers do not include private parties, private photo shoots, school events, and corporate parties. With these large crowd numbers, the possibility and probability of an accident occurring is very high.

Pros of Having Insurance	Cons of Not Having Insurance
Shows that you are a professional Santa	You will be personally responsible for anything and everything that goes wrong.
Contracts May Require Business Insurance	
Provides a layer of defense against claims	
Limits your liability	
Provides protection for your family	

Terms of Insurance

Aggregate — Maximum amount an insurer will reimburse a policyholder for all covered losses during a set time period, usually one year.

Customer Injuries — If a customer is hurt in an accident involving your business, general liability insurance can help pay for medical expenses.

Damage To Premises Rented — Protects you if the property you are renting for your event is damaged, to include fire damage.

Damaged Customer Property — General liability insurance can cover expenses to repair or replace customer property accidentally damaged by a business.

Excess Liability Insurance — Type of policy that provides limits that exceed the underlying liability policy. It does not broaden the stated coverage but will provide higher limits on top of the original policy. The primary purpose of Excess Liability insurance is to close coverage gaps and to offer an added layer of protection in case the underlying insurance is exhausted of all resources.

General liability Insurance —Covers third-party lawsuits (those coming from people outside of your company), including slip-and-fall accidents, product liability, property damage to third parties, and reputational damages.

Group Coverage — An insurance company provides a limit on how much money is set aside to cover claims from a particular group. Once the group exceeds this cap, no more insurance claims are paid. At that point, the individual now has the responsibility. This allows for a lower priced premium.

Group Policy — Insurance that covers a group of people such as the members of a society or professional association.

Individual Policy — A policy in which an individual or entity receives financial protection or reimbursement against losses from an insurance company.

Medical Expense — Covers medical costs incurred for treatment of injury.

Occurrence — Covers claims made for injuries sustained during the life of an insurance policy, even if the claim is filed after the policy has been canceled. It is your responsibility to keep a copy of your insurance policy past its expiration date.

Personal & Advertising Injury (additional cost) — If someone sues a business owner or employee over slander, libel, or copyright infringement, general liability insurance can help pay for legal expenses.

Premium — A policy's premium is its price, typically expressed as a monthly cost. The premium is determined by the insurer based on you or your business' risk profile, which may include creditworthiness.

Policy Limit — The policy limit is the maximum amount an insurer will pay under a policy for a covered loss.

Product Liability — Not all property damage or customer injuries happen inside a store. If a business manufactures, distributes, or sells products, it can be sued over the harm its products cause to people or property.

Sexual Misconduct Liability — Sexual misconduct and molestation liability insurance is a specialty form of coverage. It is specifically designed for business owners and was developed to provide protection against the financial losses and the damaged reputation that can be associated with sexual misconduct or molestation allegations.

Theft Losses — Covers Santa equipment that is stolen.

Insurance Provisions — When one party agrees to maintain certain types and levels of insurance coverage or add another as an additional insured on a policy.

Commercial General Liability Policy — Provides coverage for liability assumed under certain contracts if the liability meets the other terms and conditions of the policy. The individual policy for a business must be examined to be certain of what is or is not covered. It is important for all businesses to follow best practices in their contractual relationships. In most contracts, there will be indemnity provisions, insurance provisions, and/or waiver clauses.

Indemnity Provisions (also known as "hold harmless" clauses) — When one party promises to reimburse another party, and in some cases defend the other party, for the other party's losses or claims - sometimes without regard to fault.

Waiver, Release, and/or Subrogation Waivers — Designed so that one party cannot sue or seek redress from the other party.

Example of Certificate of Liability Insurance

ACORD® | **CERTIFICATE OF LIABILITY INSURANCE** | DATE (MM/DD/YYYY) — Date of Policy

THIS CERTIFICATE IS ISSUED AS A MATTER OF INFORMATION ONLY AND CONFERS NO RIGHTS UPON THE CERTIFICATE HOLDER. THIS CERTIFICATE DOES NOT AFFIRMATIVELY OR NEGATIVELY AMEND, EXTEND OR ALTER THE COVERAGE AFFORDED BY THE POLICIES BELOW. THIS CERTIFICATE OF INSURANCE DOES NOT CONSTITUTE A CONTRACT BETWEEN THE ISSUING INSURER(S), AUTHORIZED REPRESENTATIVE OR PRODUCER, AND THE CERTIFICATE HOLDER.

IMPORTANT: If the certificate holder is an ADDITIONAL INSURED, the policy(ies) must have ADDITIONAL INSURED provisions or be endorsed. If SUBROGATION IS WAIVED, subject to the terms and conditions of the policy, certain policies may require an endorsement. A statement on this certificate does not confer rights to the certificate holder in lieu of such endorsement(s).

PRODUCER — *Insurance Company* Agent/Broker who issued the insurance policy.

CONTACT NAME / PHONE (A/C, No, Ext) / E-MAIL / ADDRESS

Name of Insurance Company Offering Coverage — INSURER(S) AFFORDING COVERAGE — NAIC #

INSURED — *Name of Insured/Organization* Santa's legal name

INSURER A / INSURER B / INSURER C / INSURER D / INSURER E / INSURER F

COVERAGES — CERTIFICATE NUMBER: — REVISION NUMBER:

THIS IS TO CERTIFY THAT THE POLICIES OF INSURANCE LISTED BELOW HAVE BEEN ISSUED TO THE INSURED NAMED ABOVE FOR THE POLICY PERIOD INDICATED. NOTWITHSTANDING ANY REQUIREMENT, TERM OR CONDITION OF ANY CONTRACT OR OTHER DOCUMENT WITH RESPECT TO WHICH THIS CERTIFICATE MAY BE ISSUED OR MAY PERTAIN, THE INSURANCE AFFORDED BY THE POLICIES DESCRIBED HEREIN IS SUBJECT TO ALL THE TERMS, EXCLUSIONS AND CONDITIONS OF SUCH POLICIES. LIMITS SHOWN MAY HAVE BEEN REDUCED BY PAID CLAIMS.

INSR LTR	TYPE OF INSURANCE	ADDL INSD	SUBR WVD	POLICY NUMBER	POLICY EFF (MM/DD/YYYY)	POLICY EXP (MM/DD/YYYY)	LIMITS	
X	COMMERCIAL GENERAL LIABILITY						EACH OCCURRENCE	$ 1,000,000
	CLAIMS-MADE [X] OCCUR						DAMAGE TO RENTED PREMISES (Ea occurrence)	$ 100,000
X	Abuse/Sexual Molestation						MED EXP (Any one person)	$ 5,000
							PERSONAL & ADV INJURY	$ 1,000,000
	GEN'L AGGREGATE LIMIT APPLIES PER: POLICY / PROJECT / LOC						GENERAL AGGREGATE	$ 3,000,000
X	OTHER Per Member						PRODUCTS - COMP/OP AGG	$
	AUTOMOBILE LIABILITY							$
	ANY AUTO						COMBINED SINGLE LIMIT (Ea accident)	$
	OWNED AUTOS ONLY / SCHEDULED AUTOS						BODILY INJURY (Per person)	$
	HIRED AUTOS ONLY / NON-OWNED AUTOS ONLY						BODILY INJURY (Per accident)	$
							PROPERTY DAMAGE (Per accident)	$
								$
	UMBRELLA LIAB OCCUR						EACH OCCURRENCE	$ 1,000,000
X	EXCESS LIAB CLAIMS-MADE						AGGREGATE	$ 1,000,000
	DED / RETENTION $							$
	WORKERS COMPENSATION AND EMPLOYERS' LIABILITY Y/N ANY PROPRIETOR/PARTNER/EXECUTIVE OFFICER/MEMBER EXCLUDED? (Mandatory in NH) If yes, describe under DESCRIPTION OF OPERATIONS below	N/A					PER STATUTE / OTHER	
							E.L. EACH ACCIDENT	$
							E.L. DISEASE - EA EMPLOYEE	$
							E.L. DISEASE - POLICY LIMIT	$
X	Worldwide coverage			Policy Number - QWER12345	07/01/2009	07/01/2019		

DESCRIPTION OF OPERATIONS / LOCATIONS / VEHICLES (ACORD 101, Additional Remarks Schedule, may be attached if more space is required)

Santa portrayal by insured member XXXXXX XXXXX effective XXXXXXXX. Certificate Holder is included as an Additional Insured with regards to General Liability Coverage includes "Abuse and Molestation" within the limits of $300,000 per occurrence/500,000 aggregate for this member. This coverage only applies with acceptable background check that is verified and on file.

CERTIFICATE HOLDER — *Certificate Holder* Should be your legal name

CANCELLATION

SHOULD ANY OF THE ABOVE DESCRIBED POLICIES BE CANCELLED BEFORE THE EXPIRATION DATE THEREOF, NOTICE WILL BE DELIVERED IN ACCORDANCE WITH THE POLICY PROVISIONS.

AUTHORIZED REPRESENTATIVE — Signed by representative of insurance company

© 1988-2015 ACORD CORPORATION. All rights reserved.

ACORD 25 (2016/03) — The ACORD name and logo are registered marks of ACORD

Annotations:
- Policy Form — Claims made or per occurance.
- General Aggregate — This indicates the coverage limit for policy.
- Limits of Insurance — Should be equal or greater to limits on your policy

Charitable Work

As you spend time in the Santa Community you will come across Santas who prefer to do mostly charitable work which is highly admirable. These Santas truly have the heart and passion to share the joy of Christmas to those who are sick, disabled or in hospice care. These Santas give of themselves, which is the true meaning of Christmas.

For most Santas, there is a mix of payable and non-payable (i.e., charitable work). Yes, by taking a charitable position, you do have to give up a paid visit request, but the work is the most rewarding. Remind yourself that you must always remain humble and remember not to ever take for granted the magic of the Red Suit.

Keep in mind, that there is a need for Santas to donate their time for non-profits in any town. If you don't know where to start, look up your local social services office and ask for orphanages, abused and battered spouses and children's homes and homeless shelters. If you want to donate your time, contact the local police and fire departments because many times they are collecting food or clothing to distribute at Christmas for local needs or for organizations.

Military Veterans

Amidst the Santa community there are Santas who have served or are currently serving in the military, and thus are aware of additional opportunities to volunteer time as Santa. Many Santas overlook the possibility of working with federal government agencies as part of their Santa career. Whether you are connected directly to the military, or just have the desire to help our military families, you can reach out to military base activity coordinators and military support organizations.

The Department of Defense (DoD) and The Veterans' Administration (VA) have undertaken an outreach effort to identify small businesses owned and controlled by veterans and service-disabled veterans. You can find the application process on the VA website.

Here are the basic qualifications: (1) veteran; (2) business license; (3) business checking account; (4) registered with the state (5) insured; (6) Data Universal Numbering System (DUNS) number; (7) operating agreement showing veteran runs 51% or the top paid employ) ee of the business; (8) registration in System for Award Management (SAM) program; and/or (8) disabled service-connected veteran.

There are two distinct types of contracting businesses that Santas can apply and compete for under the VA. The VA has created two different categories for veterans to apply for Veteran-Owned Small Business (VOSB) and Service-Disabled Veteran-Owned Small Business (SBVOSB).

The process is time consuming but well worth it in the long term in addition to the certification, you can include the images on your page once you are certified.

Santa Schools

When it comes to Santa schools, it's truly based on your personal choice and finances. Before you commit to a school, evaluate your current Santa character. There are over 30 different schools and workshops which have been advertised in 2022. Due to the considerable number of Santa schools that pop up after each Christmas, there are too many Santa schools to list in this book. Be aware that most of the new schools that come out are designed and taught by Santas with less than ten years of experience in the Santa community.

Personal note: Honestly, I fell into that trap. I thought I needed to attend every school that was offered locally. The answer is "no." I learned more about researching the Santa community with my mentors Phillip Wenz, Dutch Schrap, and Thomas "Tom" Sheerin, than through a school. You will learn more from close mentors than listening to a Santa on the internet spewing their thoughts and feelings about the Santa community. I found that most schools will only teach you bits and pieces of the information. As of the publishing of this book, there are no schools that teach how to completely set up a Santa Claus business or the history of the Santa community. To be quite honest, the schools are more of a networking source than anything else.

When evaluating a school, take some time to do some research on the instructors. Find out where they have worked as Santa and if their regular employment have any additional impact on being Santa. Find out what other students think about the school. Then ask yourself: "What will I learn?, Can I learn most of this from a book or YouTube™?" Be honest with yourself and select a school which will meet as many of your needs as possible.

Just remember that most Santa schools are more a social gathering than an actual training environment.

Pricing Your Services

Each year, Santas from around the country start asking on the Facebook groups, what should they charge for their services, and how much are they worth to make someone else happy.

As part of the Santa community, you need to ensure that everyone follows the law. It is against the law for a group of individuals to set a price for any particular or specialized service. There are Santa groups or individuals that may make you feel pressured to comply with their prices in order to keep the average market price high. Remember this goes against the Racketeer Influenced and Corrupt Organizations (RICO) Act of 1970.

Basically, the RICO Act prohibits competitors to fix prices which is illegal, whether prices are fixed at a minimum, maximum, or within some range. Illegal price fixing occurs whenever two or more competitors agree to take actions that have the effect of raising lowering or stabilizing the price of any product or service. When consumers make choices about what products and services to buy, they expect that the price has been determined freely based on supply and demand, not by an agreement among competitors.[11]

With that said, pricing for each Santa will be different for multiple reasons. A typical annual income for a Santa will range from $5,000 to $25,000 per season depending on the clientele.

Several items factor into the pricing of your visit:

> 1. Your location will be the biggest contributing factor to determine your price (time/distance to clients).
>
> 2. The average income for your locality.
>
> 3. The condition of your Santa suit; leather belt; Santa boots?
>
> 4. The number of years that you have been portraying Santa.
>
> 5. Your long-term costs to maintain and replace items as needed and ongoing costs such as maintaining a webpage and covering insurance policies.

Typically, real bearded Santas will generate more money, however, recently there has been a push towards the traditional bearded Santas. Many photographers are more interested in hiring the traditional bearded Santa for their photos.

One of the best ways to determine how to set your price for the upcoming year is to check the following sites to find out what the Santas are charging in your area:

1. GigSalad (www.gigsalad.com)
2. The Bash (aka Gig Masters) (https://www.thebash.com/entertainer)
3. The Bark (https://www.bark.com/)

There are a few types of services that you might wish to think about before you set and advertise your prices:

— Photography sesssions
— Phone call from Santa
— Video Call from Santa
— A letter from Santa
— A quick 15-minute visit with Santa with gifts for a single family.
— A 30-minute visit and/or 60-minute-long visit for the family
— Adult Party
— Homeowners Party
— Christmas Eve visit and/or Christmas Day visit

Freelance Santa

Yes, there is a huge pay gap between the mall/department store rates and the private business rates. The reason why this pay rate varies so much is because there is no baseline on what the prices should be. Honestly, everyone is going to set their own prices. The average price per hour for the freelance Santa is approximately $150 per hour.[12] A mall Santa averages $37.68 per hour.[13]

Personal note: Every summer, I sit down to figure out my pricing for each one of my venues: Home Visits, Business Visits, Photography, and Christmas Eve. Something also to consider is an out of season rate for your photographers. I prefer to do more photography work in the fall, so I have more time to make home visits during the Christmas season.

The charts below are what I use each year to figure out my costs. Remember, most of these items listed in the charts are tax deductible from the Schedule C tax form. It's simple and to the point. This is a baseline of what you need to break even this tax year.

Examples of Long-term Expenses

Long Terms Expenses	Initial/ Replacement Cost	Estimated Life of Item	Cost Per Year	Estimated Gigs Per Year	Use of item per Gig
Halco Suit	$400	4 years	$100	15	$6.67
Boots	$135	5 years	$27	15	$1.80
Suspenders	$50	7 years	$19	15	$1.27
Yak Hairpiece	$500	2 years	$25	15	$1.70
Leather Belt	$135	7 years	$66	15	$4.40
Business Cards	$100	2 years	$50	15	$3.33

Examples of Annual Cost

Items Purchased Annually	Cost	Cost per year	Estimated Gigs Per Year	Use of Item per Gig
Professional Dues	$40	$40	15	$2.67
Insurance	$240	$240	15	$16
Background Check	Varies by Agency	Varies	15	Varies
Cleaning of per Traditional Beard	$150	$150	15	$10
Gloves	$36 per dozen	$72	15	$4.80
Dry Cleaning	$100	$100	15	$6.67
Beard Bleaching	$200	$200	15	$13.34

Tally up all the expenses and divide it by the number of gigs you have, this will inform you of how much you need to cover your expenses for the event. Then add your hourly fee. You now have your hourly fee for the event.

Santa's Information Kit

Wow, you just received a phone to come down to the local store for a Santa Claus interview. What do you take with you? It seems just like yesterday; you went out for your first job interview. We will explore a couple of items to take on your interview.

First of all, you will need a portfolio folder. We would recommend a folder that can hold the normal size clear plastic sheets (8.5" x 11") and has inside pockets for loose leaf paper. You can pick up one of those at any store. Take your time and pick out one that fits your taste. The best time to purchase one of these is during the back-to-school specials that the stores run in July and August.

If possible, take the time to scan these documents into digital form so if you are completing an online application, you can upload and attach documents as requested. Another suggestion is to review your portfolio after every Christmas to adjust, remove and add items as necessary to keep your portfolio fresh and up to date.

Below is a list of items to place in your portfolio folder:

- Any newspaper articles/magazine articles about you as Santa
- Photos of you with and without children
- Business Card
- One-page resume
- Letters of reference
- Santa Schools or related classes (costume, makeup, hair, etc.) attended
- Business License
- Completed W-9 Form (This form gives the business your SSN/TIN.)
- Background Check
- Copy of your liability insurance
- Your hourly rate
- Statement explaining your reasons for portraying Santa – For example: What made you want to be a Santa? How might you give back to your community?

After you have your meeting, follow up a week later to inquire if there are any questions. Be polite if they decide not to hire you.

Santa Claus Oath

In order to create an industry standard of ethics, Phillip L. Wenz in October of 2008, wrote the Santa Claus Oath on the ideals how to a Santa should act. The oath has eight principles. The oath is completely voluntary, given and received. For more information, please contact https://santaclausoath.webs.com.[14]

I will seek knowledge to be well versed in the mysteries of bringing Christmas cheer and good will to all the people that I encounter in my journeys and travels.

I shall be dedicated to hearing the secret dreams of both children and adults.

I understand that the true and only gift I can give, as Santa, is myself.

I acknowledge that some of the requests I will hear will be difficult and sad. I know in these difficulties there lies an opportunity to bring a spirit of warmth, understanding and compassion.

I know the "real reason for the season" and know that I am blessed to be able to be a part of it.

I realize that I belong to a brotherhood and will be supportive, honest and show fellowship to my peers.
I promise to use "my" powers to create happiness, spread love and make fantasies come to life in the true and sincere tradition of the Santa Claus Legend.

I pledge myself to these principles as a descendant of St. Nicholas the gift giver of Myra.[15]

Ethics

Santa should always be ethical in every decision and action. At no time should he stray from being Santa, or all that Santa represents. Santas must agree to adhere to basic standards to provide consistency across all aspects of this special work.

Santa must maintain a Holly Jolly Policy at times:
— Most of all, we are Santa for the children, not the money.
— Everyone is treated with respect and dignity
— No discrimination based upon gender, race, color, religious beliefs, national origin, age, disability, appearance or sexual orientation - especially with elves and reindeer.
— We should respect and support other Santas personal beliefs and views.
— We should not infringe on other Santas business opportunities or poach other Santas' clients.
— Santa must be above reproach. No lewd comments, gestures, or touching.
— Keep politics away from your Santa business.

In order to understand your own moral compass, you must understand why you are doing the task. Ask yourself: What is your motivation for being Santa? Is it only for money? Is it to bring hope and joy to others? Or just plain kindness?

Major Types of Ethics

Deontology Ethics are derived from one's adherence to moral rules or duties that have been established by God and the church. Those who perform the bulk of charitable work in their communities usually fall into this category based on their belief system of the *Holy Bible*. The Book of John provides a foundation in Chapter 13: "A new command I give you: Love one another. As I have loved you, so you must love one another. By this everyone will know that you are my disciples, if you love one another."[16]

Another type of ethical thinking is ***Teleological morals***. The easiest way to explain this is to say that the ends justify the means. Santas who follow this line of thinking cause problems among the Santa community because their actions are based upon money or fame. These individuals will go through the motions of caring about children, but only superficially because it justifies their goals of making money.

The third group of ethical values is called ***Virtue Ethics.*** This is a group of individuals whose belief is that they can influence others in positive ways, changing the hearts and minds of the ones with whom they engage. Most Santas would agree that showing kindness and generosity encourages others to do the same.

Concluding Thoughts

Going from the idea of becoming a Santa to initiating the set-up process with a tax ID number, business name/domain, researching and developing your Santa character and backstory details, business model, business bank account, liability insurance, tax record keeping, costume and accessories, marketing strategies, social media presence, setting prices - all the way to your first performance as Santa is a life-changing decision! Taking it one step at a time will help minimize any obstacles and allow you to enjoy this journey. Keep your eyes on the end goal of creating a sense of wonder and magic for your clientele and know you are bringing joy into the world around you.

Chapter 2

Santa's Marketing Plan

"Christmas is not a date on a calendar. It's more than a state of mind.
It's a condition of the heart."
– Toni Sorenson

Santa's Market Plan

Market Strategy

The Santa business is no different than any other business. Your business will rely on referrals and advertisement. Remember that referrals are 100% free.

Advertisements, no matter what format you use, will cost you either money and/or time. For the most part, social media is a free and effective way to create awareness about your business. We will discuss social media in a later part of this book.

There are several types of advertisements that you can purchase such as business cards, direct mailings, websites, and advertising space in the print and online editions of both local newspapers and magazines. One of the best advertisements that you could have: A positive story on the local television station.

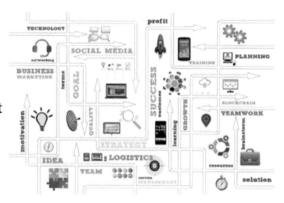

Types of Advertising

Branding/Trademarking your business

When trying to decide whether to brand or trademark your business or not, you should choose something that will make others think of you. Remember that once you use that logo, you need to use it from that time forward. Everyone will remember you by that logo. Consider the possibility of using a local graphic artist to create your logo, especially if you are concerned about the quality, creativity, and professionalism of the logo. If you think you need to hire someone, do a search on the internet for professional freelance graphic designers. The logo is used on anything and everything that you print, or post and it will keep the name of the business on everyone's mind.

Hanging up business cards/flyers

Sounds old-fashioned, but for $35 you can post a lot of information in some rather unique places. Decades ago, places like gas stations, grocery stores, and restaurants had community boards where you could hang business cards or flyers. While not as commonly found today, you can still see such community boards around grocery stores, coffee shops and local store-front windows, where the general public can view event posters and business cards. This is a quick and straightforward way to advertise that is relativity inexpensive.

Business Cards

Even in today's world, a business card is still a way to communicate with a client. So many times, we are told in the business world to have a fifteen second elevator speech about ourselves when applying for a job. We have to think the same way when we are looking for business as Santa. A way to make into a business is through the good old business card.

Now remember to keep the business card down to the basics. Only cover enough information to pique the interest of the recipients.

Second, ensure the information on the card is legible. No funky fonts, and no fonts that are too small, too fancy, or distorted. To do so is a quick way for someone to lose interest in your card and your business.

Third, make certain you have a phrase to jog someone's memory. Something catchy or something that would trigger a jog down memory lane. If you have created something already for your website or social media, then include that on the card. If you are unsure about this, think about major consumer brands and phrases you hear or see in the product's advertisements.

Fourth, get your cards professionally printed. Spend the money to make the impression. Your future customers will see that you are a professional, not a second-rate amateur. With all the printing options available, you can find in person printers or use an online printer. Shop around for cost – some places will charge more, but with other places the more cards you buy, the less the cost.

Fifth, design the card for your audience. Make the card speak for you. Persuade the recipient to want to call you or visit your website.

In order to accomplish the items listed above, follow the checklist below:

— Logo
— Company name
— Tagline or catch-phrase
— Your Santa Name
— Sleigh Number or Toy Workshop Number
— Website (if you have one) and Social Media page information
— Santa Email address

Social Media

In today's world, social media for any business is the most current way to conduct business. Almost 2/3 of consumers use social media instead of the phone to find a business. With this fact in mind, using social media for any business has become an essential part of marketing plans.

Just by having your business listed on a social media with a write-up and photos increases your business potential. The question for any business is which site you should use to promote your business. That is truly up to you. Read carefully through the next section for more detailed information about social media and websites and how to incorporate these into your Santa business marketing strategy.

Social Media and Websites

As Santa, the question is always raised...Do I need a website, or should I rely completely on social media? To honestly answer that question, we will provide you the answer to your question. In many cases, it is essential to maintain both a website and social media sites to boost your online presence.

Limiting yourself to only a social media presence on the platforms is a big risk to take once you are an established entity. If you are low in funds, free accounts on social media could be the best way to generate business in the beginning. However, as time progresses, having your own business website provides additional ways to advertise your services. Here is the case for utilizing both entities for your business to survive.

Here are some suggestions for your Social Media Marketing plan:

User Generated Content/Comments — Ask your customers to post their photos and reviews on your webpage, as well as on other online platforms, tagging your business name. These types of comments can heavily influence other potential customers.

Videos — Request that your clients post their videos of your event with them on your webpage. Ask them to tag you so it shows up on your Facebook™ wall. If you feel comfortable, do a live Facebook™ event on your page! Additionally, you can create a YouTube™ channel to promote your business using client videos or self-promotional videos.

Ad Campaigns — Google™ and Facebook™ Ads. Depending on your market this might be the way to advertise your business. Yes, you do have pay for this service separately. Google My Business™ is another great way to promote your business on the internet. Rest assured each one of these advertisement programs will cost you some money but should produce at least moderate results/inquiries.

Email Marketing — The email marketing service is great if you have an email list that you can use. As you build your business, remember to ask your clients for their email address and their permission to send them information regarding future events. Always ensure that you obtain their permission: Otherwise, you could find yourself in trouble with the Federal Trade Commission. It is possible that the company hosting your website may offer you an email marketing tool. However, if not, you should be able to find free email marketing tools on the internet that are either free or have comparable features.

Facebook™ Advertising — Over two million businesses advertise on Facebook™ as it is an inexpensive and effective way to market your business to virtually any audience. You can target your audience based on gender, age, and location. With your business Facebook™ page, you can post your logo, business card information, event calendars, online contact information, post pictures from events (as legally permissible), quick videos and reviews. You can even request to post your business information/services on local community pages on Facebook.

Yelp™ is similar to the Yellow Pages™, but instead of the book format, it is online. This is another free service where you can list your business. It is strongly recommended to set up an account; however, you will be flooded with phone calls from Yelp™ trying to sell you additional advertisement packages. One thing to mention: According to surveys, customers do use this database when searching for businesses. Also, customers do write reviews so be prepared to handle this aspect.

Google AdWords™

Google AdWords™ is a paid service. You buy an ad with certain keywords that describes your business and then you pay each time someone clicks on the ad. In a nutshell, you use key words on your page which a consumer would be looking for related to your business. For example, "Santa" would be a key word to locate a Santa and possibly use the name of the area you live in, to help consumers narrow down location.

When looking at any platform, there are always several options offered at various costs. Try using the free services first before committing yourself to any payment plans. Basically, research what services you think you will need and provide yourself with options to increase or expand services as your business grows.

In summary, the upside of email marketing service includes low cost, global reach, ease to setup, automatic "unsubscribe" feature and immediate communication. The downside of an email marketing service: the cost of email service, building an email address list and time to write the email.

The following table reveal the Pros and Cons of each social media platform

	Free Email Service	Paid Email Service	Facebook™	Google Adwords™	Google My Business™	Instagram™	Twitter™	Website	Yelp™	YouTube™
Free to Use	X		X		X	X	X		X	X
Usage Fees		X		X	X			X	X	
Set-up Cost				X				X		
Paid Ads				X	X	X			X	
Training Videos Available	X	X	X	X	X	X	X	X	X	X
Owner Control	X*	X*	X*					X*	X*	X*
Provider Control	X**		X**	X**	X**	X**	X**		X**	X**
Allow to Customize		X*						X*		
Searchable on Web			X		X			X		X

*Depends on the restrictions placed by the website/email servers   ** Must abide by hosting sites requirements

Uses of Social Media

So, why is there a need to be on social media as Santa? In today's world, social media for any business is the most current way to conduct business. Almost 2/3 of consumers use social media instead of the phone to find a business. With this fact in mind, using social media for any business has become an essential part of marketing plans.

Just by having your business listed on a social media with a write-up and photos increases your business potential. The question for any business is which site you should use to promote your business. Social media is said to be one of the most stress free but profitable platforms, with the least amount of money spent in advertising. Whether you take advantage of social media and business webpages is truly up to you.

Why social media is important:

Improved Awareness That You Exist as Santa — Social media allows you to connect your business with potential clients. In other words, you can network without leaving your home.

Cost-effective — This is an inexpensive way to advertise. Set up a business page on Facebook™ and you are ready to go. Share some photos and post events where Santa will be attending.

Engage with Your Customers — Always get your customers to engage with you at events and then online with posts and reviews. This allows customers to share their enjoyment with Santa with others, including sharing you with their friends and family.

Improved Brand Loyalty — By having a social medial presence your customer base can look you up and follow you, share you with their friends and family, provide positive feed back, or support you by personally attending or sharing details of your events.

Healthier Customer Satisfaction — Social media allows your customers to post comments and thus allows you to respond quickly. This encourages positive communications between you and your customers, thus increasing brand loyalty.

Having discussed why social media is important, the restrictions of social media need to be covered so you can see why social media should not be the only online presence you should have.

Social media sites limit the following:

Limit Customization — Social media platforms limit how much customization you can do on your platform. Every business page is very similar in the way the page is structured; there is no way to stand out from the other sites on social media.

Exposure to the Public — This is both a curse and a blessing at the same time. If someone writes a negative review, that review is there for the world to see without giving you a chance to work it out. You will need to quickly respond, offering an explanation and/ or request private communication to resolve the posted issue. Hopefully, either you or the client can then post that the issue has been resolved, which essens the overall impact of that negative review. If the review is positive, it is a blessing.

Lack of Ownership – Remember - you do not own your site on social media. You are subject to the rules and conditions that the social media platform requires for your page. If you decide to leave that platform, you will have to rebuild your presence from scratch on a new platform. Choose your social media platforms carefully and be sure to read all the rules before initiating an account.

Uses of Websites

Now it's time to talk about Websites. Why should you maintain a website with so many free social media platforms? Is having both social media and a website an overkill on maintaining an online presence? To answer these questions, here are the pros and cons of maintaining a website.

Control
You can custom build your page, making it highly personalized. This includes layout, content, color, and so much more. Each hosting platform provides different options. Shop around to find what works best for you.

Marketing Freedom
With a website you have total control over how you communicate with your customers. You have the ability to launch a customer loyalty program or advertise a limited time offer at any time. However, you are bound by the terms and conditions imposed by the website platforms on how you conduct your business.

Availability
Your business can be seen all day, every day around the world. Customers can check out your service and contact information, when you are not sitting at your desk answering social media questions.

Searchable and Available
Your website is totally searchable on the worldwide web. Yes, you may have to do some tweaking of the key terms on your page in order to raise your ranking on the search engines, but you can get help on how to do that.

The downsides of maintaining a website:

Cost — When you purchase a website, you purchase not only the website domain name, but you must also pay someone to host your page. Your domain name should be your business name. (See the earlier business section). Thus, once you purchase your domain, you will have to find a hosting company to put it on the web. Setting up your page should be easy to do. Once the page is set up, you must maintain access to your page, even if you do not do much with that page.

Additional Help May Be Required — If you are unable to create your page, you will have to hire someone to develop your page for the internet. Keep your costs low. Keep it basic as long as you can so you understand all your options.

Understanding Web Terms

Optimization
One of the biggest tools on the market is the SEO (Search Engine Optimization). Basically, you need the right information in the right place for any search tool to be able to find your particular page. Spend some time on your own to learn how to do this as you can save significant money down the road. You will optimize the most name/service recognition for the least amount of money by investing time to find the right website host, page template and inserting key/buzz words.

Static
Websites are static pages which provide a general overview of what you have to offer. The websites lag in providing real-time information on your event.

Domain Name for your Business
Simple suggestion on picking your domain page: Have it match your business name. It's one ofthe easiest marketing strategies, and by doing so, your clients will have a point of reference to reach out to you. A website domain name that matches your performance name equals continuous advertisement.

Always explore your options on picking your website host page (commercial site that host your page). Building your own website is relatively easy if you are willing to have someone sit down and show you tricks and tips to do it. While GoDaddy™ provided the answers for the author's needs have found for us, there are many sites out there from which to make this personal choice.

If you decide to have a webpage developer build your page as well as host, ensure you remain the owner of the domain! Otherwise, when your contract is up with the website developer, you could lose your control of your domain name. Another word of caution: You must be allowed to have the password of the site to maintain control of the page. If you do not have the password, you will not be able to do what you need to do to maintain/update the site and you may wind up struggling forcontrol over what gets posted and when, or worse- seeing the host remove or post items from your site.

Designing and Using Websites and Marketing Sites

When writing your overview or "About" section, focus on your "elevator speech".
— How long you have been a Santa
— Types of visits you can provide
— What clients can expect from your visit
— The Visit – how long, hourly rates, and what geographical areas you visit
— Special Skills

Edit Your Page
— Check for grammar and spelling mistakes.
— Have consistent spacing between words and paragraphs.
— Keep it simple short and sweet.

Working on Your Page
— Ensure you don't have any broken links on your page.
— High Quality Photos: Recommend 3 — 10 photos
— Try to include at least 1 video.
— Display your assortment of services and personality in photos and videos.
— Showing your positive interaction with children and adults.

Reviews are Key
— Users pay attention to "reviews of any product or service" they purchase.
— Verified reviews tend to more heavily influence purchases.

What not to include
— Crying baby photos
— Fuzzy, low-quality or outdated photos
— Avoid "ALL CAPS" and **ALL BOLD**

Note: The following information outlines basic descriptions and business applications of various social media and websites. Please refer to the Appendix sections for details on how to set up accounts and term definitions.

Facebook™ is the most popular social media network, and every business should have a Facebook™ page including Santa. When used correctly, a Facebook™ page can be invaluable to small businesses. Use Facebook™ to share everything from photos to important company updates. With a business account, you have access to powerful advertising tools not just for you, but the business that hire you for an event. On Facebook™ you can highlight information such as your contact information, hours of operation, your calendar of events, and you can advertise.

Instagram™ is another social networking site which can promote your business and personal life. Instagram™ is a free online photo-sharing application where you canupload photos and very short videos. This discussion will focus solely on Instagram™ from a business aspect. A business account allows you to add a phone number, email address and physical location. In addition, a business account allows you to advertise or promote your business.

Twitter™ is another social networking site you can use to promote your business and personal life. Twitter™ is not an application which can work effectively for every business. Twitter™ is yet another platform that users share their information within 260 characters. This section will describe how to use Twitter™ from a business aspect.

How is Twitter™ different than Facebook™?

For instance, Twitter™ is public domain by default, where everyone can see your posts until you lock them down. Facebook™ allows you to select a more private default sharing setting so that not everything is seen by anyone and everyone. If you prefer privacy, Twitter™ will probably not be the platform for you and your business.

Consequently, the news media uses Twitter™ to share rapidly developing news stories. In the same way, Santa can use this platform to share information about his arrival at a particular place. With a series of quick Tweets, Santa can easily build anticipation and excitement as he travels from the North Pole to the client's location/event.

Google My Business™ is one of the easiest ways to increase traffic for your business. It provides the simplest methods of directing traffic to either your website or Facebook™ site. This platform is a combination of an online directory listing and a social media profile. Customers can post reviews on your business.

Using the guided directions on the website (see Appendix A), you should find that the set up for Google My Business™ is a straightforward process. One of the best points about this service is that it is free, and this allows your clients to easily find you as they engage the Google™ search engine.

YouTube™

One of the easiest ways to keep videos about your business accessible to the public is on YouTube™ If you follow the guidance provided by YouTube™, this an inexpensive way of advertisement. Potential clients will be able to search via YouTube™ itself or by Google™, or follow links embedded into your business webpage or other social media accounts. Photos are a great marketing strategy, but videos allow potential clients to actually watch how you engage as Santa. For this reason, be highly selective about what you post or allow others to post!

Ways to Advertise Off the Internet

While online advertising is extremely effective, remember that there are many other ways to market your Santa business. Offline methods can also be highly effective and in some measure be combined with your webpage or social media. Do keep in mind how much you want to spend for advertising/marketing and that you need to keep excellent records on how clients found your business, so you know where to reduce and where to increase your marketing expenses. The upside of an email marketing service includes low cost, global reach, ease to automate, automatic "unsubscribe" feature and immediate communication.

Join Local Business Groups — A fantastic way to promote your business is to join a local business group. Business groups can range from a loosely knit group of business owners that get together for breakfast once a month to a more organized group such as the local business association of a town or a county.

Partner With Other Businesses — Combining your efforts with another business or two can significantly increase business for all involved and the popularity of an event.

Personal Note: For instance, I worked with two other businesses for an event, and it was a big hit. I combined a visit from Santa with a restaurant and local artist which allowed each business to reap the rewards of attending the event.

Speak At Events — In terms of branding and establishing yourself as an authority, few things are more impactful than being a speaker at popular events in your niche. While invitations to speak at larger events are often extended because of accomplishments or visible influence, you can also work your way into these opportunities by becoming a talented speaker through delivering great talks at smaller events. Practice speaking with your "Elf" as a critic or videoing yourself before your event.

Or you can simply use it as another marketing channel by speaking at some of the following types of events/organizations:

- Local clubs –Rotary, Lion's, Chamber of Commerce
- Business networking groups
- Specific interest clubs (photography, hiking, sewing, etc.)
- Browse local events on Eventbrite.com and Meetup.com
- Schools; Churches; Boys and Girls Club
- Check events in your local newspaper and magazines
- Big companies and their employees

Return on Investment

At the end of each season, ensure that you have collected data from your customers on how they found you. This is valuable information that can help you choose how to advertise for the upcoming season more effectively.

Budget

For a business to be successful, you must plan for your advertisement expenses. You must figure out how much you plan on spending on business cards, websites, and other types of advertisement. Include these expenses on the chart I provided on Page 22 which will allow you to figure out the price of your services. Be advised that sometimes webpage services are cheaper when you purchase a longer contract.

Notes:

Checklist: Social Media and Business Webpages

Here is a list below for your use to monitor, update and respond on a daily, weekly, and monthly basis for your social media accounts.

Daily	
	Ensure you reply to incoming messages.
	Check to see if anyone has tagged you on a photo and consider whether to use the photo/mention on your timeline for advertisement on Facebook™.
	Ensure your Facebook™ /Twitter™ /Instagram™ followers know where your public events will be.
	Schedule posts according to effective times of day: ☐ 2-3 times daily for Twitter™. ☐ 2-5 times daily for Facebook™. ☐ 1-2 times daily for Google+™. ☐ 1-3 times daily for Instagram™.
	Always post original content to your social media: blogs, videos,podcasts, etc.
	Engage with active followers and fans.
Weekly	
	Connect with your followers.
	Check analytics and adjust scheduling and topics as needed.
	Create and monitor weekly goals for engagement, consistency, growth.
	Update your list of publicly scheduled events.
Monthly	
	Check all social platforms and consider needed adjustments to scheduling, topics
	Schedule postings as allowed by the social media platform.
Semi-annual	
	Schedule postings as allowed by the social media platform.
	Set goals and reminders for the next month.
	Check all social platforms and consider needed adjustments to scheduling, topics, etc.
Annual	
	Evaluate what worked and what did not work.
	Do a master plan on what postings will go on each social media platform.
	Set goals and reminders for the next month.

Monthly Checklist for All Aspects of Santa Business

I have created this handy check-off list for you to consider during the year. Please take this list, look it over, and modify it to fit your needs. Please only copy for your personal use.

As Soon as Your Christmas Season Ends or January	Completed
1. If you hired contract help during the Christmas season, mail out 1099-Misc. so it arrives at the IRS office before January 31st.	
2. Write "thank you" notes to your clients.	
3. Make a list of all your successes and failures.	
4. Ask your clients if they are willing to provide positive comments about you on your Social Media pages.	
5. Properly store your suit/dresses and related items: heavily padded hangers, use desiccant (moisture reducing) packs near your garment bags.	
a. Prepare your suit for long-term storage. After you have it cleaned for the season, place it in a breathable bag in a cool, dark room/closet. If your fur is detachable, remove it from the suit and store in a cotton bag. This allows your suit to breathe and cuts down on dust.	
b. Inspect your White Gloves - remove any that are stained, dingy, or need repair.	
c. Clean your belt. Take some time to put a thin layer of wax on your belt.	
d. Clean your boots and shine them (keeps the dust from accumulating). Put some type of fresh smelling items inside your boots. You can stuff the boots with paper to keep the shape of the boot or use a water noodle. I have found that the round water noodles are the best to keep the shape of the boots in the off season. You can cut them to fit the size of your boots.	
e. Check the heels of your boots/dress shoes for uneven wear. Repair or replace boots/dress shoes as needed.	
6. Test all equipment before storing. Clean, repair, and replace, as necessary. Make a list to ensure you know what you need in advance and can start shopping for those items.	
7. Replenish supplies or make a list of the supplies that you will need during the next season. After Christmas sales are a great source for bargains.	
a. Great time to buy "giveaway items" for next year (clearance items; coloring books, stickers, pencils, etc.)	
b. Make a list of makeup that you need to replace.	
c. Replace makeup brushes	
8. Last-Minute Tax-Deductible Purchases:	
a. "Thank you"" gifts for services that supported your Santa such as your dry-cleaners, booking agents, hair-dresser, etc.	
b. "Thank you" gifts on sale/clearance for the next year.	

As Soon as Your Christmas Season Ends or January (Continued)	Completed
9. Evaluate your materials, procedures, and props used during the season. See if you need to replace or discard elements from your performance. Do a complete inventory of items and decide if you need to repair or replace them in the current calendar year, or, wait until the following tax year to make the purchase.	
10. Update your online Santa profiles on Facebook™, Instagram™, Twitter™ (and any other social media sites) and your website with your most recent photos and information.	
11. Make a list of everything you would like to do and purchase for the upcoming year.	
12. Make a list of "dream jobs" you would like to work for the next Christmas Season. Develop a plan on how to reach out and sell yourself to those businesses.	
13. Check for any reviews or posts on your social media sites. Acknowledge the posts and clear up any negative issues immediately.	
14. Gather your tax documents, receipts, and records.	
15. Remove batteries from all electronic devices before storing.	
16. Create a Master Calendar for the upcoming year.	
17.	
18.	
February	Completed
1. Update your website with latest information such as this year's rates and update your resume, photos, and videos.	
2. Update and order new business cards.	
3. Start planning out your master calendar.	
4. Contact last year's clients for this upcoming year's books.	
5.	
6.	
7.	
8.	
9.	

March	Completed
1. Review your financials; begin preparing for taxes.	
2. Hire a seamstress or tailor to make needed repairs and alterations to current suit or to create any new suits, shirts, or accessory items so that it is ready for potential "Christmas in July" gigs.	
3. Continuously update your Master calendar throughout the year.	
4. Start attending yard sales/flea markets/thrift stores for props.	
5.	
6.	

April	Completed
1. File your taxes. According to your tax situation find out what expenses you were allowed to deduct or not. Strive to keep better records for this upcoming year.	
2. Develop and/or brush up on your Santa routine for the upcoming season.	
3. Continuously update your Master calendar throughout the year.	
4. Attend yard sales/flea markets/thrift stores for props.	
5.	
6.	
7.	
8.	

May	Completed
1. Reach out to businesses about "Christmas in July" opportunities.	
2. Develop and/or brush up on your Santa routine for the upcoming season.	
3. Continuously update your Master calendar throughout the year.	
4. Attend yard sales/flea markets/thrift stores for props.	
5. Contact local chamber of commerce to find out if they need a Santa or Mrs. Claus for their 4th of July parade.	
6.	
7.	

June	Completed
1. Reach out to businesses about "Christmas in July" opportunities.	
2. Develop and/or brush up on your Santa routine for the upcoming season.	
3. Continuously update your Master calendar throughout the year.	
4. Attend yard sales/flea markets/thrift stores for props.	
5. Send reminders to previous clients to start booking early.	
6. Continue to check in on your social media sites.	
7.	
8.	
9.	
10.	
11.	

July	Completed
1. Ensure you are hydrated for your "Christmas in July" events.	
2. Contact local photographers in your area. (If you notice a photographer is working with a Santa, please do not bother the photographer, RESPECT each other. You don't want another Santa contacting your photographer and taking your business.	
3. Continuously update your Master calendar throughout the year by taking reservations.	
4. Attend yard sales/flea markets/thrift stores for props.	
5. Send reminders to clients to start booking early.	
6. Review your Christmas shopping list and start shopping.	
7.	
8.	
9.	
10.	
11.	

August	Completed
1. Starting reviewing the latest toy list for the year on the popular store sites.	
2. Develop and/or brush up on your Santa routine for the upcoming season.	
3. Continuously update your Master calendar throughout the year by taking reservations. Send reminders to clients to start booking early.	
4. Attend yard sales/flea markets/thrift stores for props.	
5. Update your Christmas card list.	
6. Review your Christmas shopping list and start shopping.	
7. Start reharsing your routine.	
8. Pay for your liability insurance.	
9. Order your background check.	
10.	
11.	

September	Completed
1. Continuously update your Master calendar throughout the year by taking reservations. Send reminders to clients to start booking early.	
2. If you use a traditional beard set, check your hairpieces for damage and ensure they are washed and styled properly.	
3. Check your suits	
a. Check your fur	
b. Check for missing snaps or buttons.	
c. Check your boots for rot/cracks/cleaning/uneven wear	
4. Ensure your makeup blends work with your skin tone and order make-up if needed.	
5. Inspect and replace your make-up brushes and applicators as needed.	
6. Ensure you have enough white gloves for the Christmas Season. (Rule of thumb: one pair of gloves per day/per event).	
7. Visit the doctor and ensure your immunization shots are up to date. (Shingles; Flu; and Pertussis shots).	
8. Ensure your Christmas card list is up to date. Start signing and addressing Christmas cards on your list.	
9. Continue to review the latest toy list for the year.	
10.	
11.	

October	Completed
1. Continuously update your Master calendar throughout the year by taking reservations. Send reminders to clients to start booking early.	
2. Plan your holiday time with your family (i.e., cooking, visiting, etc.).	
3. Update your website and social media accounts.	
4. Get your vehicle ready for the busy season by getting it inspected; serviced; and ensure your vehicle insurance is up to date for the season.	
5. Polish your brass buckle.	
6. Update your Nice Book with all your current clients.	
7. Test your props prior to start of your Christmas season.	
8. Finalize business arrangements that are already on the books and secure all the retainers.	
9.	
10.	
11.	
12.	
13.	
14.	
15.	
16.	
17.	
18.	
19.	
20.	
21.	

November	Completed
1. Continuously update your Master calendar throughout the year by taking reservations.	
2. Create a calendar of events on Facebook to show potential clients where you will be for public events. Pull the information from your master calendar. Keep it updated daily.	
3. If you are a real-bearded Santa, ensure you have scheduled a haircut and bleaching session two weeks before your first Christmas appearance.	
4. Update all your social media accounts and website.	
5. Before the Christmas season starts, please ensure you have completed the following tasks:	
a. Update your Christmas Card List. Address your cards, sign them, put postage on them, and mail them by Thanksgiving weekend.	
b. Start wrapping your presents.	
c. Schedule and have quality family time.	
d. Sit down and plan out your Christmas Day with your family.	
e. Start decorating your home, office, and vehicle and complete it by Thanksgiving.	
6.	
7.	
8.	
9.	
10.	
11.	
12.	
13.	

December	Completed
1. Continuously update your Master calendar throughout the year by taking reservations.	
2. Up your calendar of events on Facebook to show potential clients where you will be for public events. Keep it updated daily.	
3. If you are a real-bearded Santa, ensure you have scheduled a haircut and bleaching session during the Christmas season.	
4. Update all your social media accounts and website.	
5. No drinking alcohol 12 hours before being Santa/Mrs. Claus for an audience. If you are a traditional bearded Santa, the rule of thumb is no alcohol 24 hours prior to an event.	
6. Keep nourishing snacks and bottled water in your bag or car.	
7. Stay hydrated.	
8. Get plenty of sleep.	
9.	
10.	
11.	
12.	
13.	
14.	
15.	
16.	
17.	
18.	

Concluding Thoughts

There are many decisions to be made regarding your Santa business. Take time to consider your family and day-job situation when considering whether to work as a mall/department store Santa or to book individual events/visits. Then consider your business budget as well as your time constraints while you explore possible social media, business webpages and other online marketing tools. Do your research and be prepared to start the business earlier enough in the calendar year that you can have things set up, materials purchased and book events without trying to crunch so much into too short a time. Review the checklists on the following pages as a guide for timely decisions. Find what works best for you and do not be afraid to start off small, especially your first Christmas season.

Chapter 3

Communicating with Children

Faith is salted and peppered through everything at Christmas. And I love at least one night by the Christmas tree to sing and feel the quiet holiness of that time that's set apart to celebrate love, friendship, and God's gift of the Christ child.
– Amy Grant

Communicating with the Children

Sometime during your Santa career, you may be asked to write a letter to a child from Santa. Yes, there are plenty of sites on the web that can send a letter to a child: However, you might be asked by a parent, friend of the family, or even your spouse to write a special letter to a specific child.

I have included instructions over the next several pages on how to write a Santa letter and seal it. If you have time and are creative, make your own Santa Certificate for a child to be on the Nice List. Please try and see what you can accomplish on your own before hiring a professional to do it for you. There are plenty of examples on the internet if you do the research.

Letter from Santa

A letter from Santa is one of the most important things a Santa can do for a child. Spend some time reviewing sample letters on the internet. Do not copy any letter from the internet because that letter could be copyrighted, and you could face severe criminal and civil penalties. If you want to use something already made on the internet, you can opt to purchase templates or look on the internet for copyright/free public domain sites for templates.

Try developing your own letter before purchasing and downloading someone else's design. You can make it simple or complex depending on your creativity. Always save an original template of your letter, so it is ready to modify and print when needed for that special child. Keep it handy as the Christmas season approaches.

Nice List Certificate

Develop a "Nice List Certificate" for your clients. The joy of a child seeing their name on a certificate that certifies that they are on the Nice List is very important, just as important as the Nice List Book. You could hire a graphic artist under the "Work for Hire" contract. Otherwise, you might be able to find a certificate template online available to purchase which you can modify for each client. If you are hand printing the child's name, practice writing the name so you can center it onto the certificate. Learning how to do basic calligraphy could be an added bonus for hand printing.

Note: Always verify the spelling of a client/child's name! Having your name misspelled is never fun and it takes the joy out of the moment. This could cost you future business opportunities.

Envelope

If you have some time, take a moment and design the envelopes for the letters and the "Nice List Certificate". This just continues to add to the magical and uniqueness of the moment, rather than putting special documents into a plain, boring manilla envelope. Also, consider using an envelope large enough to hold the document without having to fold the document in case the family wants to frame it.

Personal Note: My family and I had fun designing the letter size and the 8.5 x 11 size envelopes. We made it a family affair. There are plenty of online websites which offer royalty free images that you can modify for your own custom design.

Using Wax Seals on Santa Documents

Wax seals add authenticity and sentimental charm to your Santa documents such as the Santa Letters and the Nice Certificates. Complete Wax Seal kits can be purchased on suppliers' websites such as Amazon and eBay for an economical price.

The following are the pros and cons of three different types of wax applications:
— Traditional Wax Stick (contains wick)
— Wickless Wax Stick
— Wax Beads

It is recommended that you spend some time practicing the application of the wax seal. To save money, practice placing the wax seal on aluminum foil, parchment baking paper, or a silicone baking mat, then re-melt the wax in the melting spoon to use again.

Traditional Wax Stick (contains wick)

This low-cost method of creating a wax seal is a shortcut method which always ends-up creating problems. The user cannot see if enough wax has been used to create the actual seal. The application of a direct flame or traditional wicked wax will result in an undesirable amount of charring and will inevitably stain the wax black.

Wickless Wax Stick
Using sealing wax without sticks is the most traditional style of sealing wax.

Using Wax Beads

When using traditional 'wax beads' it can be difficult to judge how many pieces you need to make one seal. Using this method is considered the most economic. Personal note: In our experience, we have found that that one pebble is enough to make one seal.

Self-Adhesive Wax Seals

You can also purchase wax seals that are pre-made with the Santa seal. This will save you time, but these items can range between $0.75 to $2.00 each. You just remove the paper tab from the back and place it on the envelope.

Other Methods of Communication

While written letters and certificates are unique and create special memories, Santas are sometimes called upon to use other means of communication with children. If you have ever watched *The Miracle on 34th Street,* you saw Kris Kringle using sign language and speaking in multiple languages with the various children coming to visit him in the department store. Just think of the joy and the smiles you can bring by taking the time and effort to learn a few signs and phrases, just as that famous Santa did in the movie. In fact, it could be to your benefit along with the clients to ask in advance if anyone is hard of hearing, or has limited English, so you have time to practice. People greatly appreciate such efforts.

In Appendix E, you can find the basic sign language alphabet and a few Christmas words. In Appendix F, I have included common Christmas phrases in Spanish.

Visits, Events & Related Technology

As Santa you will make visits which may include a wide range, from children's private parties, to parades, to store events, to business holiday parties to veterans' homes to senior care homes, so that you work with senior citizens, children of all ages, special needs children and adults with various disabilities. You may discover that you excel working with such a broad range or with a particular group. You may do the bulk of your visits in person, but also might do many virtual visits. Here are some tips and reminders of how to successfully work with various groups and ages, whether in person or virtually.

How to Have a Smooth Home Visit

Now that you have established your Santa business and are getting inquiries for surprise home visits, as Santa you need to ensure a successful visit with the families and businesses. While this type of event focuses on Santa, Mrs. Claus and the elves might be helpful to have with you.

What to expect at a home visit: Santa needs to remember that every home visit is different, but there are some standard items to be covered in a visit:

> — A special entrance from Santa

> — Meet and greet

> — Photo opportunities

> — "Chair time" with both kids and adults

> — "Questions and Answers" with Santa

> — Performances such as storytelling, or a book reading for which you have permission to read such as the original The Night Before Christmas.

> — Handing out gifts

> — A hearty goodbye and magical exit

Things to do before you visit the family:

As Santa, call and discuss details with your family host/organizer. This could be their first sleigh ride and they may have questions. By calling, you can modify the visit from your normal routine. In addition, any questions the host/family may have could potentially yield a wealth of information and ideas that could help you.

Ask key details about the event.
As Santa, you will need to know the following:
> How many people will be there?
> What are the names of the children and ages?

Remind the host, that Santa is old and sometimes will forget an important fact or name. However, to ensure that does not happen, it is best to have someone introduce each child by name and age as the child approaches Santa's chair.

Share special considerations. Santa needs to know if there are any special needs prior to his visits. Also, it is best for Santa to know about any language barriers. Another thing to consider is whether there are any cultural considerations of which Santa should be aware and understand.

Make sure Santa can get in! Ask if the location is inside a gated community, and if so, ask the host to either share the access codes and/or add Santa Claus to the access list. Make certain you have directions to the location ahead of time. If you are unfamiliar with that area, ask the host about typical traffic issues so you can plan sufficient travel time.

Stay in communication. Santa needs the cell phone number of a designated helper at the location. This allows Santa to text that person prior to arrival and will facilitate Santa in making his grand entrance. Prior to the event, you should check your phone and the designated helper's cell phone to see they are fully charged.

Check to find out if there has been any sadness or loss. If there has been the recent passing of a loved one, or someone is currently stationed overseas, it is best that the host makes Santa aware of this prior to the event. In addition, if someone is missing from the event, Santa could offer to record a special message for that person.

Ask where Santa's sleigh will be allowed to park. Remember that parking is important, especially since you are traveling from home to home. Ask your family or host if they can reserve a space for Santa. One great method is to ask the host to put a sign out saying, "Reserved for Santa." Be certain that guests do not notice you prior to entrance or after your exit, so that children do not ask about your version of Santa's sleigh.

Check the location of Santa's chair. Take charge, Santa, and recommend to the host to put your chair next to the Christmas tree or a well-lit background. Santa may know that not to sit next to a roaring fire since you are already warm in your suit, but the host may not think of this.

Prepare your seating arrangements. During the phone call, ensure Santa will have help once he enters the location to find his designated seat. As Santa, you should suggest a chair that has a strong straight back and without arms, preferably a dining room table chair with a pretty Christmas sheet or blanket covering it. Side note: Santa should remember to keep his feet flat on the floor while someone is on his lap.

Ask about the background noise. Remind the host or family that having background music on at a lower volume will ensure that the children and adults will be able to hear Santa talking, while still providing a special mood. Santa has important words of wisdom to discuss before and during the big event.

Take photos first. Explain to the host that it is in the best interest of everyone to get the photos with Santa completed as soon as Santa walks in the door. After that everyone can relax. If the host insists on photos with pets, have them provide a clean blanket to place on your lap because you must keep animal fur and dander off your suit. [See "Paws with Claus" section.]

Check the timing of passing out gifts. Ask the host where the gifts will be when you arrive. If the gifts will be outside, ensure that they are in a large plastic trash bag with some type of marking. Make sure that they will fit in Santa's bag in advance. If there are too many gifts, have your elf or the host help you. Request that the host write the child's name with a permanent marker directly on the wrapping paper. Labels always end up falling off in Santa's bag. A great suggestion is to remind the host to have a few back up gifts in case someone shows up unexpectedly. Go with the flow of the host/family as to pacing for unwrapping the presents.

Santa Claus Reminders for the Visit

Get paid. Remember though - Santa never collects payment from the host in front of the children. Do your best to have the payment paid in full prior to the event.

Santa assumes all children are on the Nice List.

Santa should politely decline any food or drink, or if someone insists, take nothing beyond a few nibbles. A bottle of water with a straw is always welcome.

Santa should not drink any alcohol. Remember, Santa must drive the sleigh and manage eight reindeer.

Always ask for a great review, referrals and ask permission in writing to use photos from the visit.

Sneak and Peak

Ideally, this happens after the children have nestled into their beds on Christmas Eve night. Arriving about 30 minutes after their normal bedtime works well.

There are several options to consider for this visit, so it is best to coordinate with the parents to find out what they are desire. Here are two of the best options.

OPTION 1: This is a home visit where the family hides from Santa and observes him working. This is when Santa fills the stockings and places the presents under the tree. Santa could take a nibble of a cookie and "drink his milk."

The parents need to ensure that the children do not interact or speak with Santa...they only watch. Santa pretends that he doesn't know they are watching. He tries not to look at them. This could last anywhere from 10 to 30 minutes depending on the family. Try planning for 15 minutes to have enough time to set everything out, but not so much time that the children forget to be "awed" and start trying to engage with Santa.

OPTION 2: Parents who do not wish to wake their children up can film/video Santa Claus unloading gifts, filling stockings, eating cookies, etc. When the children are awake on Christmas morning, the parents have proof that it was Santa who came and left gifts for the children, and not the parents.

Special Needs Visits

Sometime in your Santa career, you will get a phone call for a home visit for a special needs child.

Personal note: I personally know that most Santas thrive at delivering a top notch visit for the child. I have no doubt that you will be able to do the same.

Here are a few common disorders that you might experience:

Autism — Autism is a disorder of neural development that is characterized by impaired social interaction and communication, and by restricted and repetitive behavior. There is a wide spectrum of autistic children, including some who are nonverbal.[17]

Asperger's Syndrome (AS) — Those with this disorder characteristically have poor social interactions, obsessions, odd speech patterns, and peculiar mannerisms. Kids with AS often have limited facial expressions, have difficulty reading others' body language, may engage in obsessive routines, and often have sensitivity to sensory stimuli. Kids with AS display many of the same characteristics as those with high functioning Autism. Noise impact children with this condition.[18]

Attention Deficit Hyperactivity Disorder (ADHD) — Children with ADHD are often hyperactive and have difficulty focusing or paying attention for long periods of time. There are many variations of ADHD, some tied to aggressive behaviors and trouble fitting in socially. [19]

Cerebral Palsy — This is a group of disorders that affects a person's ability to move and keep balance and posture. Cerebral palsy is the most common motor disability in childhood. Cerebral means having to do with the brain. Palsy means weakness or problems with using certain muscles. Cerebral palsy is caused by abnormal brain development or damage to the developing brain which affects a person's ability to control his or her muscles. The symptoms and functioning of each person with cerebral palsy varies. Cerebral palsy does not get worse over time, but the exact symptoms can change over a person's lifetime. [20]

Down Syndrome — An extra chromosome is the key cause of Down's Syndrome. Chromosomes are small "packages" of genes in the body. They determine how a baby's body forms during pregnancy and how the baby's body functions as it grows in the womb and after birth. You will often find that a DS child is extremely friendly and affectionate. [21]

There are many different areas of special needs, including the ones outlined above, as well as disorders such as a child who is blind, mute or has a speech impediment. Each disability has unique challenges. Upfront dialogue with the child's parents or guardian is the best way to learn how to interact for a child who may require special attention.

Now for the essential part....Did you know that you are legally responsible not to discuss the child's medical issues outside your visit? You are bound by Health Insurance Portability and Accountability Act (HIPPA) when portraying Santa. According to the CDC website, "a person or organization using or disclosing individually identifiable health information to perform or provide functions, activities, or services for a covered entity" is responsible for maintaining the person's privacy. [22]

A great resource for information on Special Needs for Santa is:

Santa America – https://www.santaamerica.org

Here are a few tips to help you through the visit:

Time and Planning – When the parents or caregiver calls to make an appointment for Santa to visit, ask the parents if there are any concerns that you may encounter. Develop a game plan with the parents. Explain what you usually do during a home visit. Ask the parent(s) or caregiver for their input and then plan out the flow and timing of the visit. Just remember a little advanced planning can go a long way.

Don't Force Communication With the Child — The autism spectrum refers to a range of disorders. Some of these disorders have common traits, such as the struggle to communicate. Remember to keep your sentences short and concise. As a business practice avoid sarcasm because most autistic individuals are typically very literal about everything you say.

Respect Their Desire for Personal Space — Anyone that has autism normally experiences sensory overload from stimuli that most individuals would generally find comfortable. These children may not want to be touched at all, including hugs. In fact, this can lead to the equivalent of a panic attack for them. Kindness should be shown in other ways, such as verbal praise or small gifts.

Stay Calm — To help keep a child with autism calm, speak softly and allow the child to have their own personal space. Raised voices increase tension and panic.

Keep Things Consistent — Ask the caregiver to ensure that the room that you will be in as Santa is kept in its normal state, or as close to it as possible.

Guard Against Sensory Overload — Please ask the caregiver to remove anything that could cause a sensory overload before your arrival. Have the caregiver provide a presentation or book about Santa before you come to visit.

Enlist Parents — Please ask the parents to help guide you and the child to a mutual understanding of what will happen during your visit. Always follow the parents lead. (They will have to pick up the pieces once you have departed).

Be Prepared — Ask questions prior to your visit, follow the plan, and allow for plans to change as needed to assist the child. Always be prepared for unexpected, especially if the child feels challenged, which could cause/trigger a meltdown.

Senior Home Visits

Every year, millions of our senior population enter senior citizen living facilities. For most of them, it is a time when they can no longer care for themselves physically, emotionally, or mentality. Normally most senior facilities do try to celebrate three holidays each year – Mother's Day, Father's Day, and Christmas. (Other holidays might include 4th of July, Veterans Day, and Thanksgiving Day.)

A visit from Santa brings hope and cheer to the residents during a time when many families will not be able to visit them. Most of the residents will enjoy your Santa visit.

Key points to remember:

— Speak clearly and a little slower than you usually would

— Still be lively in your discussions with the residents

— Be attentive to each resident's wishes (active listening)

— Let the residents lead you in a Christmas song

— Never enter a room without permission of the staff or the resident

Most of the time, Santa will do these visits as a charitable contribution to the community.

Corporate Parties

Corporate Parties are commonly known as "Adult Parties." This is a decision that you will need to make upfront with your Mrs. Claus as to whether you will attend/work these parties.

Normally this type of event involves adult type of activities which usually include alcohol and other adult behaviors. It is your responsibility to ensure that you always maintain your professionalism at these parties. As Santa, these parties require you to be more outgoing. You cannot just sit in your chair. Rather, it is expected that you mingle with the guests.

If this is truly a business party, do your homework on the business. Research their webpage and find out who the President and Vice President are of the company. Then, be certain that you make yourself available to them during the party. As you get ready to depart for the night, always check out with the host/hostess and ensure that you make a last visit around the room before you leave.

Being a Mall Santa

Historically, mall Santas did not appear on the scene until the end of World War II when many new homes were built in subdivisions outside the big cities. The developers were quick to create shopping centers and regional shopping malls. Since many families left the inner city in droves, so Santa also moved from the downtown department stores to the local shopping malls.

Most mall Santas work for a photography company for the duration of the Christmas season. As a mall Santa, be prepared to sign a legally binding contract covering the terms of your employment and how you will conduct yourself both on and off the photo set. Many malls start their Santa sessions as early as mid-November and continue until when the mall closes on Christmas Eve. On condition that you honor your contract, you are guaranteed employment for this timeframe. One of the downsides of being a mall Santa is if your relief Santa is unable to come in for his shift, you will then have to stay for the remainder of the day which means you could miss your other scheduled events for that day. Some Santas decline this type of employment to have the freedom to accept any events which fit into personal/professional calendars. Others prefer the steady schedule of a mall Santa, without pursuing additional events.

During the 1970s the average pay for a mall Santa was in the $3 to $5 range per hour. In 2019, according to CNBC™, the hourly median rate for department stores and malls was $37.60 per hour. In a recent study conducted by CNBC™, the average income for Santas dropped in 2019. Several of the main reasons why the pay went down: (1) Malls are closing, and the photography companies pay what they offer. (2) There currently is a surplus of Santas in several major metropolitan areas. (3) As this book was written, Noerr Photography and Cherry Hill Photography merged, reducing the competition between mall photography businesses. (4) Currently only Amusematte and Cherry Hill photography remain.

Rules for Santa to Remember about Mall Photography

— Santa should **NEVER** engage in high pressure sales of a photograph of the child and himself.

— Always have the parent place child on your lap.

— Your job is to is to give each child your undivided attention to answer the ever important questions from the child.

— During your time as a mall Santa, it is important for you to show the photographer that you are not a prop for their photo. Be engaged during the photo session.

Department Store Santa/Big Box Store Santas

Most department stores and big box stores hire Santas every year to entice mom and dad into the store. Yes, to sell products. Santas need to understand that you are there to entertain the children while the parents look at merchandise on the shelf.

Many of these department stores will hire out to a talent agency or agent to fill these slots. Usually, these positions run from Veterans Day Weekend right up until the store closes on Christmas Eve, which amounts to about 550 hours per season. Most department stores will only allow a Santa to work 6 hours per day, with less than 40 hours per week, in order to keep you as a part-time employee. In some stores, you are considered an Independent Contractor. Most of these stores will require you to sign an agreement that will allow them to make you work on your off-duty time with no additional compensation.

When working for a department store, remember — the store will take care of their customers before they take care of Santa. You must also remember that for any store "time is money." To bring families into the store, most stores will offer free photos with Santa, arts and craft projects, refreshments, along with other events or activities.

With that being said, the pay is not the best. On average in 2018, the pay was between $30 to $38 per hour – which is about the salary of a mall Santa. You are expected to be on stage for 50 minutes of every hour. You can expect payment to be higher on different days of the week; Saturday is usually a slightly higher paying day than a regular weekday.

So here is a quick breakdown on how it works:

You are subject to a non-disclosure agreement regarding your employment at the store.

During your time as Santa during the 40 to 45 day run, you could have up to 30,000 visitors, including the furry animal members of the family.

If you are an "out of town" Santa, normally your transportation and housing costs are covered in the contract by the placement agency.

Typically, there is one lead Santa for the store. The lead Santa makes the schedule. Then everyone else is given the opportunity to choose the hours which best fit their schedule.

If your replacement Santa is late, you are required to stay until he arrives. It is written in the contract of the department stores/big box stores that you are required to remain until released at the end of your shift, whether it ends as scheduled or adds unscheduled extra time. This could impact your after-hour Santa visits/events.

Santa Travel Bag

Once you start planning your season, it is important to have 2 (two) Santa Travel Bags. One should be in your vehicle and one in your home in case anything happens. Having two similar travel bags allows flexibility in case a situation arises that you cannot access the other regular bags. This list is not
all-inclusive, but a good reference from which to start.

☐ Information Sheet about your Visit	☐ Toupee Glue/Strips
☐ Cell phone that has GPS	☐ Bottle of Liquid Adhesive
☐ Extra pairs of Santa Glasses	☐ Rubbing Alcohol Wipes
☐ Extra pairs of Santa Gloves	☐ Safety Pins
☐ Extra Santa Hat	☐ Beard Balm
☐ Santa's Magical Key	☐ Mustache Wax
☐ Comb	☐ Lip Balm
☐ Brush	☐ Extra Pair of Clean Socks
☐ Toupee Glue/Strips	☐ Extra Santa Suit
☐ Hand Sanitizer	☐ Extra Santa Boots
☐ Hand Towel	☐ Extra Santa Belt
☐ Duct Tape	☐ Extra Santa Buckle
☐ Sewing Kit	☐ Water Bottles
☐ Money ($20 in $1 dollar bills for Tolls)	☐ Toll Road Pass
☐ Water Bottles	☐ Mouth Mints
☐ Dog Whistle for Pet Photos	☐
☐	☐
☐	☐
☐	☐
☐	☐
☐	☐
☐	☐
☐	☐
☐	☐
☐	☐
☐	☐
☐	☐

(You may make a copy of this page for your own personal use)

Parades

When working a local parade, first find out who is responsible for the float you are riding on and who oversees the individual float, as well as the parade itself.

1. Key Contacts — Always have a complete list of parade officials and municipal staff who will be involved in the event planning and permit process and who are the people organizing the parade. These contacts should include:

— Parade organizer
— City/county manager
— Police contact
— Fire Department

2. Regulations and Requirements — Ensure what is required of Santa before submission of permit applications and inspections. If Santa and his crew are responsible for Santa's float, ensure that you follow the rules and regulations of your local community for the float's design and function. Also confirm whether you or your elves toss candy canes to children along the parade route.

3. Written Safety Plan and Emergency Response Plan — Ensuring you have a written safety plan is critical for addressing emergencies. This plan could, amongst other things, address risk mitigation and contingency planning; safety briefings for event participants and other stakeholders; driver and vehicle screening; safe float operation. Be certain your plan includes inclement weather and emergency/security responses. All parade drivers and officials should have a copy of these plans.

4. Route — Make certain you have route maps and emergency detour maps which clearly delineate street closures. Be sure you know where the stationary performance zones are located. It is your responsibility to walk the parade route prior to the performance to ensure you become familiar with the parade route.

5. Vehicles — The local police department should be able to advise you the safe speeds for transporting your float and safe distances to maintain between your float and the group/float in front of you.

6. Driver's Requirements — Ensure the driver has a current driver's license. Discuss the required safe speed and distance with the driver before the parade begins. Clarify any concerns the driver may have preferably prior to the day of the parade.

7. Participants — If you are not in charge of your float, get to know your float crew. Otherwise, you need to ensure that you follow all the local requirements such as participants under the age of 18 may require an additional chaperone.

8. Assembly and Disassembly Area — It is important to know where the assembly and disassembly sites are located for parking, loading, and unloading parade vehicles. Always have a plan for removal of debris in the disassembly area. You might consider writing a Thank You note for your driver and float crew, and the parade organizers in advance to hand out at the disassembly area.

9. Viewing Stands and Distinguished Visitors — Designated viewing areas are useful to direct performers on where to perform.

10. Insurance — Check with local officials to find out if you need to have special insurance for your performance or if the parade organizers carry insurance for all participants.

Participating in the Parade

This list is not inclusive but will provide general guidance on how Santa needs to respond to the parade crowd.

Do's

— Most of all, have FUN. You will have an adrenaline rush because the crowds will be chanting your name.

— Be on your best behavior at all times.

— Make connections with a highly skilled professional photographer to take photos or video of you along your parade route.

— Wave, smile, point at the spectators like you know them personally because as Santa, you know everyone. Be sure to interact with the crowd as much as you can along the way.

— Point to someone in the crowd and throw both arms out in front of you for a virtual hug, reciprocate the "I love you" sign language sign when a child gives it to you.

— In a smaller parade: Connect with each and every face –they are your community family. They want to experience the thrill of seeing you laughing and smiling.

— In a smaller parade: Be prepared because the audience can hear anything you say and will want you to say "Ho, Ho, Ho."

— Larger parades: The likelihood of the people along the parade route hearing you without a microphone will be very slim. Focus more on gestures and expressions if you do not have a microphone.

— Since you have done your preliminary walk through of the parade route, you should know the landmarks where the television cameras will be located. Ensure that you put your best foot forward.

— Be certain that you control your hands and gestures. You will have cameras that will photograph any out of the ordinary items. Cameras show everything! Video cameras can pick up voices at distances you would not expect!

— Make sure that you thank each one of the parade sponsors of the parade at the beginning, the middle, and the end. If you happen to see them individually, ensure they receive a hearty thank you for the allowing you to be in their parade. Offer them a photo with Santa: This will help you when they make the decision for the following year.

— Prior to the event, make sure that the parade event team knows that you are available for publicity shoots and press events for the parade. Remember to be certain the team gets a copy of those professional photos of you (taken by your own photographer) from the parade.

— Ensure you download any photos of you in the parade from Facebook™, Instagram™, Twitter™, etc. for your scrapbook and "like" the photos. If you have time, interact with the page. Make a personal connection.

— If you have a Mrs. Claus or Elf on the float, coordinate with her/him on which side of the float they prefer.

— If you are tossing candy canes, have several bags ready for each of you when you run out. Also, try to make sure the little children can get the candy since older kids often grab it all.

— If the float comes to a stop, ensure that you take a moment to pose for photos because that photo could make it to the front page of your local paper!

DON'Ts

— Don't showboat or promote your own agenda.

— Don't just wave hands in the air – connect with people.

— Don't compete with Mrs. Claus or your Elf on the float.

— Don't use rude language during the parade. If you have any gripes or complaints, do it off the set. You never know who is listening and broadcasting what you are saying on your float.

— No lewd gestures.

Notes:

When you Fill In as a Substitute Santa

Sometime in your career as a Santa, you might receive a call from another Santa, asking you to take over a Santa visit for him. You fulfill the requirement and then the family asks you to return the following year. You have a dilemma. You can accept the job for the following year, or do you take the high road and ask the family to reconsider their request.

Personal note: I have found that if you are asked by the family/sponsor that you should graciously decline. There are two reasons why you should: (1) Your integrity. Yes, Santas do talk to each other. By taking the job from another Santa, you have just put your integrity in question with the Santa community. (2) By accepting the position, you have just limited yourself of becoming a substitute Santa for someone else.

The following is a sample of a note you can use to express your thanks and your dilemma. Once the issue with the original Santa has been resolved, then you will know to either move on or if you can accept that position with a clear conscience.

Sample note:

Dear (Family/Sponsor),

Thank you so much for your kind words about my visit with your family. I had a wonderful time at your event. However, based on the situation that I need to decline your offer at this time until you have had a chance to speak with (the other Santa's name).

I believe since (the other Santa's name) was the original contracted Santa for your event, (the other Santa's name) has priority with you and your event. So, I also believe it is in the best interest of all parties involved that you talk with him first before offering me future work. I cannot take another Santa's business, especially when he was unable to fulfill his contract with you for a valid reason and would be able to return and fulfill any future work for you.

Wishing you and your family an amazing Christmas, and I hope our paths cross again in the future.

Merry Christmas,
Your Substitute Santa

How to Say "No" Being Santa
(Personal experience)

As Santa, we want to be able to be Santa to everyone all the time. We need to realize that there is only 24 hours in a day, 7 days in a week, and sometimes 4 weeks between Thanksgiving and Christmas or sometimes 5 weeks. There comes a time when Santa must say "No" to potential clients or current clients due to time constraints.

I always tell my clients that in order to book a Santa visit, I must confer with Mrs. Claus because she has the appointment calendar as well as she knows when our children and their families will be home for the holidays or there is an important event our family must attend. Saying I need to check the books gives me the time to consider if I can and should respond with "yes" or "no." It also provides a viable way to say "no" if you have had this client in the past and you know how they treated you as Santa.

So many times, I have heard from other Santas that they started out being Santa because they enjoyed the "Spirit of Christmas", but over time they must meet a certain quota of Santa visits or events to break even for the year because of all the unnecessary Santa gear they bought for the year. I know that for myself I would rather be on the negative side of the checkbook versus jeopardizing my health and safety to chase a dollar. Pace yourself with your visits and what you spend for Santa.

Then there is the other side of the coin, we all as Santas know that if we turned down a visit, we might not get the phone call next year. So, be honest and upfront: Ask the client, "May I call you when I start taking appointments for next season?" What is the worst they will say? "No?"

I have come to realize that I love working with my current clients. Yes, I do realize that at any given time I could lose these clients because the children can and will age out. This is a situation all Santas must face at times in their careers, which means missing the children you have watched growing up and always ask current clients for referrals.

We as Santas need to learn balance. We all need to understand that Santa needs to stay healthy not just for his clients, but for his own family and to manage your "day job" expectations or obligations.

You control your schedule. Don't let someone else control you.

Concluding Thoughts

Who realized Santa engages with so many people of all ages and abilities? Santa has a tremendous range of opportunities to bring joy to one and all at parades, home visits, senior citizen care facilities, community events, store events and more. Your imagination is really the limit for what you can do, and as discussed in the next chapter, you can explore virtual events, teleconference calls, photo sessions and videos! Whether you create special letters and certificates, or participate in live events, take time to be in the moment, thinking of all the happiness you add to your clients' holiday. Consider especially the anticipation of children as they come to see Santa and how you, as Santa, make that moment a reality for them; a moment which becomes a special and fond memory as they grow up.

Chapter 4

Virtual Visits and Related Technology

Christmas waves a magic wand over the world, and behold,
everything is softer and more beautiful.
– Norman Vincent Peale

Virtual Visits

The idea of visiting Santa on the internet is not completely a new idea or thought. In 2020, COVID brought this technology to the forefront for most Santas. Santas who previously could not participate due to medical issues or physical issues were now back in the game for the Christmas season. Virtual visits are affordable and personalized just as much as home visits, except having the benefit of no travel time.

The national average price for a virtual visit in 2021 was $35.00; however, prices increase as Christmas Eve gets closer. These visits last about 10 – 15 minutes.

As Santa, there are multiple decisions you will need to make if you determine to go the virtual route for your visits. The biggest decision you will make is whether you will you work for yourself or work for a "virtual visit business". There are pros and cons to doing this yourself as well as working for someone else; both are presented for review.

Personal note: I would hope that you would make an informed decision on what you decide. I have gone through the information that is currently available about this type of business and consolidated it for your review.

I would not expect "Virtual Visits" to go away in the future. The benefits of this type of visit for the family include no lengthy line to wait in; usually no screaming children; and parents can schedule the visit for their preferred time. A benefit for you would be no travel time, so you can schedule multiple visits without leaving your virtual visit set-up in your home.

In previous years, an independent Santa only had to compete with other local Santas, but now you must compete against nationwide businesses which can easily out-spend your advertisement budget. It will be your mission to establish your own repeat customer base to help your business for future years.

To prepare for the virtual visit, you will need to ensure you have everything ready and correct. Based on several hours of observing other Santas prepare for their grand performance and reading comments from other Santas, here are some pointers for your virtual visit:

Beard: Take the time to properly groom your beard. Spend the extra time to brush and style your beard. Plan to whiten your beard earlier in the season in order to ensure your beard is white as snow.

Teeth: Ensure that you have brushed your teeth prior to your performance.

Glasses: If you wear glasses, ensure that they are clean and spotless.

Gloves: Ensure the gloves are clean, like they just came out of the package.

Names/Details: When the adults arrange for a virtual visit, remember to ask for name annunciation and any key details Santa should "know" so when you appear, you are the authentic and genuine Santa they expect.

Video Studio Set-Up Links

You can use most of the same equipment from the photography studio section to make your video studio. Technology changes every couple of months, so I would highly suggest that you do some research on the internet to find up-to-date tutorials. I have listed several links to get you started on the journey.

OBS (Open Broadcaster Software) is free and open-source software for video recording and live streaming. YouTube™ has plenty of videos on how to use OBS. I would take time to explore what is out on the web since technology changes every minute of the day. Here are some subjects to search:

- How to start streaming with OBS Studio | Hardware
- How to Use OBS Studio (Beginners Guide)
- Use OBS for Video Calls
- How to Record and Stream Skype with OBS Studio
- 5 Green Screen Mistakes Beginners Make

Little Prompter – A Little Prompter is a compact, versatile, and easy to use teleprompter that helps you quickly deliver a polished video to your students, to your employees, or to the public. Up until now, teleprompters have been clunky, expensive, and difficult to operate and many required film studios or a production team. Prices tend to range from $100 - $400.

Desktop Tabletop Tripod – You can use the desktop tabletop tripod to hold your prompter and webcam.

PromptSmart™ Pro – PromptSmart™ teleprompter apps are unique because they include a patented VoiceTracktm method of scrolling the text. VoiceTrack™ uses speech recognition to scroll as you speak and pause when you pause, without the need for an internet connection, helping to reduce anxiety associated with public speaking and with video production. (https://promptsmart.com/products/pro). App for phone – Price $20.

Webcam – A webcam is a video camera which feeds or streams an image or video in real time to, or through a computer to a computer network such as the Internet. Be certain you can use the webcam with your computer and that you download the latest version. Keep up to date on the version downloads. Prices can range from $40 - $400.

Video Teleconferencing – Santa Calls

Backgrounds are an important part of any image. They set the tone and blend everything together. Depending on your background, they can provide a three-dimensional feel of the photograph or the video for your audience.

Here are some basic industry definitions of the terms used in this section:

Green Screen – The use of a single color, in this case green, as a backdrop in filming to make it simpler and easier to add backgrounds, characters or other images such as such as computerized graphics.

Proper use of a Green Screen – Stay 6 to 10 feet away from your green screen. Make absolutely certain that you do not wear anything with a green hue because anything green will disappear and you could look like you are missing body parts or part of your Santa's Workshop. Ensure that there is no shine on the subject's face from the lights.

Blue Screen – Again, this is the use of a single color, in this case blue, as a backdrop in filming to make it simpler and easier to add backgrounds, characters, or other images such as computerized graphics.

How to use a Blue Screen – When using a blue screen, you will need more light in your studio than a green screen. Remember that a blue screen is ideal for working with darker backgrounds or nighttime conditions. Avoid wearing or using items of any shade of blue.

A backdrop is a painted cloth hung across the rear of a stage or a studio.

Pros and Cons of Backdrops

The following chart visually exhibits the benefits and drawbacks of backdrops, screens, and live background displays.

PROS	Green Screen	Blue Screen	Backdrops	Real Background
Works with any camera	X			
Inexpensive	X	X	X	
Requires less light	X			
Shows more detail	X	X		
High luminance for daytime scenes	X			
Better for darker scenes		X		
Natural Appearance			X	X
3-D Look			X	X
Privacy of your home	X	X	X	
Operates in small space	X	X	X	
Color correction is easier		X		
Can make different scenes	X	X	X	
Capturing More Complex Foreground	X			
Daytime/Indoor & Outdoor Scenes	X	X	X	
Greater Chroma Key Accuracy	X			
Nighttime/Twilight Scenes		X		X
Color Accuracy Matters Most		X		
Made to Last			X	X
Wipe to Clean	X	X	X	X
Change background on regular basis	X	X		
Computer software and training needed	X	X		
Easy of setup time	X	X		

CONS	Green Screen	Blue Screen	Backdrops	Real Background
Expensive			X	X
Special Computer Software and Training	X	X		
Wrinkles in the screen	X	X	X	
Lighting Reflection			X	X
Requires Additional Lighting		X	X	X
Watch for blue hues in material		X		
Not good for nighttime scenes	X			
Could be expensive to set up				X
Harder to Correct Color Balance	X			
Most Popular Selection	X			
Very Heavy			X	X
Large to Store			X	X
Backgrounds can be expensive			X	X
Shadows				X
Fuzzy or blurry edges	X	X		
Need distance from the screen (6 to 8 ft)	X	X		
Separate Lighting behind the screen	X	X		
Sensitive to green hues	X			
Sensitive to blue hues		X		
Fragile	X	X	X	X
Expensive			X	X
Time consuming to setup			X	X

Setting up the Lighting and Background Screen
Blue and Green Screens

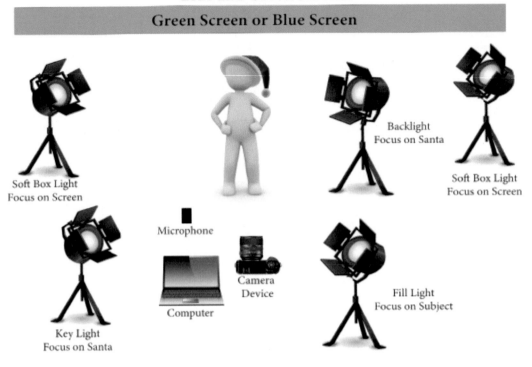

Green Screen or Blue Screen

Soft Box Light
Focus on Screen

Backlight
Focus on Santa

Soft Box Light
Focus on Screen

Microphone

Camera
Device

Computer

Fill Light
Focus on Subject

Key Light
Focus on Santa

Working with a Virtual Visit Company

In 2020, there was a dramatic increase of business ventures that offered "virtual visits for Santa". Working for a virtual visit company has both positives and negatives and certain things you should expect as part of such a business. Here is a description for some of the items to be considered as a member of a virtual visit company.

General Information:

> **Contractor vs Employee** – Most companies will list you as a contractor since it is less liability for them. As an employee, if you are on the "clock" and something happens to you such as you become injured by tripping over a cord, the company is responsible, but as a contractor there is no recourse.
>
> Ensure you have the terms of your "employment" in writing.

Positives of working for a virtual company:

Equipment – Certain companies will provide Santa a camera and computer to make the phone calls only if the Santa agrees to a signed contract of required hours.

Payment for Your Services – In this setting you do not need to worry about payment because the company you are working for will secure the payment for your services.

No Job Hunting – The company does all the promotional for this operation.

Scheduling –The company does all the scheduling for you according to your contract.

Income – You and the company decide your pay and how often. Ensure you get this in writing. Read the fine print of the contract.

Negatives of working for a virtual visit company:

Customer Lists – The company considers these lists as "proprietary information" and are owned by the virtual visit company. They record all the customer's information: name, address, phone number, and email address. The company will use that information for years to come. Yes, that includes the names and all contact information for all the clients whom you brought into this company.

Non-Compete Clause – Yes, that is right, you cannot solicit or take clients from the company you are working for, including the very clients you brought to the company.

Non-Disclosure Agreement – Plain and simple, most companies use these agreements to protect only their interests, not yours.

Fees – Certain virtual visit companies require you to use and charge for the background with their logo painted on the backdrop. Fees range up to $200.

Equipment – Certain companies will require Santa to purchase all the equipment for the virtual call such as the computer, camera, lights, and microphones.

Insurance – You will be required to pay for your own insurance.

Background Check – You will be required to pay for your background check.

Taxes – The company is required to issue a 1099 or W2 for your payment of your services.

Computer/Phone Technology

With the rise in "Virtual Visits", there was a corresponding increase in phone calls with clients. Many Santas needed to learn new terms and definitions as well as how to use new software. This section will discuss Voice over Internet Protocol (VoIP). Yes, for some Santas this is a new tool in the workshop bag.

VoIP is a technology that allows you to make voice calls using a broadband Internet connection instead of a regular (or analog) phone line. Some VoIP services may only allow you to call other people using the same service, but others may allow you to call anyone who has a telephone number including local, long distance, mobile, and international numbers.

This is a great service where you can use your current cell phone and have two phone lines come to the same phone. **Personal note:** I prefer using Google Voice™ because of this feature, but there are other companies that do provide the same service.

Google Voice™
Many Santas do not have the funds to keep a second phone line available just for their Santa business. An alternate option suggested is Google Voice™. This provides the protection that if a child calls Santa, you will have the opportunity to decline the call and let voice mail answer it for you, especially if you are not at your best.

Google Voice™ is a phone service Internet protocol (VoIP). This service has been around since 2009. You can make and receive phone calls and send text messages. The remarkable thing about this service is that you can change the phone which you are using at any time without a penalty.

Google Voice™ does have a personal account and business account feature. If you register as a personal account, it is free and will work with phone numbers in the United States. If you use it for numbers outside the United States, there is a cost. The business account is a fee-based subscription service.

Google Voice™ requires you to establish a Gmail™ account before you can use this service. If you use Gmail™ for your business email, all your contacts are automatically available for you to call from your account.

Santa and Television, Radio, and Print Media

As Santa, you must assume that whatever you do will end up on someone's social media page. If the posting gets a large interest from the public you could end up with a phone call from the local press which could include newspaper, radio, or television interviews. As Santa you must never act out of character: If you do, it could possibly end your Santa career.

Always keep your answers short and precise. Do not allow any wiggle room in your answer which the reporter could turn into a negative sound bite/quote. Gently get a "Ho, Ho, Ho" somewhere in your interview. You are Santa and the authority on Santa related matters.

When answering questions, make sure you control the discussion. You can always deflect away from the question by responding with something that does not pertain to the question. Normally the news reporter does not actually ask the questions; instead, the camera man does.

Always remain in character as Santa. Remember that Santa does not engage in political or racial issues or anything controversial.

Here are some of the typical questions asked in an interview, which you can use to rehearse your responses in advance:

Why are you Santa Claus?

When did you start this profession?

What led you to this profession?

Who is your favorite reindeer and why?

When (or how) did you and Mrs. Claus meet?

When did you and Mrs. Claus become newlyweds?

How many hours does it take for Santa to make around the world?

What is your favorite cookie?

Note: Check "The Nitty Gritty" chapter for other FAQ and responses to assist you in preparing for interviews and events.

Cameras, Photos & Zoom

Creating a Photography Studio on a Budget

Let's face it: Santas are all looking for ways to offer something another Santa is doing or not doing. Photography is a fantastic way to generate additional income without leaving your cabin at the North Pole. However, the thought of taking an existing space and converting it into a studio can be daunting to say the least! As Santa, a complete studio is absolutely unnecessary unless you are taking and processing the photos. Instead, having a partial studio allows for the flexibility for video calls.

Over the next couple of pages, you will see the bare bone basics of creating Santa's photography studio.

Camera

A digital camera is one of the most important pieces of your "studio" whether you are doing still photography or doing video calls with your iPhone™ or Android phone™. Ensure that you have a good understanding on how to operate and use the camera prior to your scheduled session. Make sure that you have a high quality with high-capacity chip for your camera and a sturdy adjustable tripod. You might also consider having a remote timer, a handheld remote, or an attached trigger if your elf or Mrs. Claus are not available to snap the picture.

Insurance

Check to be sure that your insurance will cover this type of activity whether you are shooting photos on your property, leased property, or at another location. You also need to have sufficient personal property insurance to cover replacement of all photo equipment. You also may want to get a membership to a group like Professional Photographers of America, as they provide legal assistance should legal assistance be needed. They also provide valuable information regarding a multitude of photography tips and advice.

Background Check

Please ensure your background check is up to date prior to any scheduled activities involving the general public. (Please see the section on Background Checks for details).

Printer

Only purchase a printer if you are offering instant photos; otherwise send everything to a photo lab. If you use an online service where the customer buys directly from the photography lab, ensure you receive a commission for using that service. Using a third-party online photo service can result in significant costs savings for you.

Lighting

Lighting is the most expensive single purchase in your studio other than your camera and your printer. In your studio, you will need at least three lights: an overhead, and two fill lights on 45-degree angles. The actual kit that you chose is a personal preference. Since you may need to set up your lighting kit at an event, consider purchasing a lighting kit which is easily transportable. Just make sure you purchase fluorescent bulbs with color temperatures between 3500-5000k for that natural "soft daylight" look. The ideal lighting is 5400k.

The average cost for the Lighting:

>   Lighting Kit — approximately $280.00
>   Replacement bulbs – approximately 10 @ $10.00 apiece.
>   Total: $290 + depending on the lighting kit

Backdrop System

Personal note: Since I only use our "studio" for Christmas backdrops, I purchased the low-end backdrop stands which breakdown and are easily transportable. After the Christmas season, I can put away the "studio" and return the room to a regular spare room.
Cost: $30 – $200

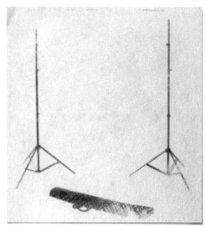

Backdrops

As for backdrops, there are numerous places to purchase the backdrop you want to use. Amazon and Wish carry backdrops for as low as $6.00. For solid colors, you may also purchase heavyweight flat bedsheets in assorted sizes. A lighter weight white bedsheet works really well with white Christmas lights on it as well. To determine the height of the backdrops that you will need, use the following information provided based on a 5'9" tall person:

5-foot-tall x 7-foot-long is great for a sitting scene.
7-foot-tall x 7-foot-long is great for standing.

Sizing Chart for Backgrounds. This chart is just for reference. Contact manufacture of your backdrop for more details.

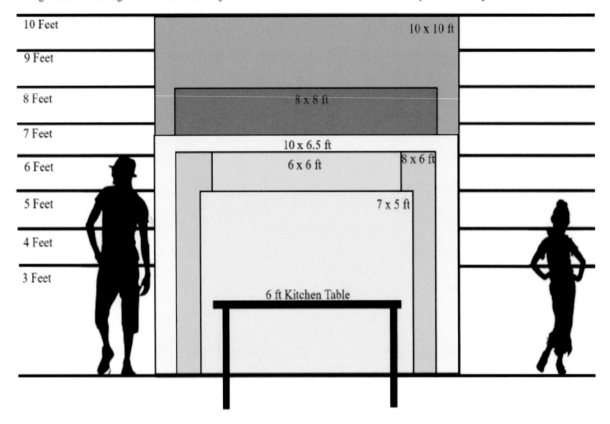

Flooring

If you are using a room in your home to cut down on overhead costs, you will need to consider not just the backdrop, but also the flooring. Most spare rooms have carpet. You need to change the flooring so that it matches the backdrop to help enhance the storyline. Here are a few suggestions to do this in an inexpensive manner.

If you put a flooring backdrop on carpet, it sinks down into the carpet below. One way to eliminate that issue is to purchase the cheapest sheet of wood (4'x8') and place it so the backdrop drapes over the wood. Then tape that part of the backdrop on the corkboard or plywood. By using this type of board, we can easily change out the "flooring" to match the backdrop.

Let's break down the flooring cost:
4 x 8 corkboard – starting around $13.00
Flooring backdrop – starting around $15.00
Total: approximate cost $30.0

Props

For props, consider using a mix of everyday toys along with Christmas props. Before you purchase any items, decide on a theme for your photo/backdrop and ensure everything used in the photo goes well with that theme. If you are looking for Christmas items, wait for them to go on sale to save money. Being mindful of how much you spend on the little items provides the money to use for the more important expensive items.

Prop cost depends on your taste, source of materials, and available sales. Also keep in mind that you will need to replace items periodically and to have props appropriate for various age ranges.

The Studio

An ideal place to use in your home is an empty bedroom. This gives you a place to set up and experiment prior to the Christmas season, and later storing that equipment. The room will need to be large, or at least long, enough to set up a camera on a tripod with sufficient space for the backdrop, props, and lighting.

Personal note: That's what we did. We put in place a plan to use a room in our home a year out, so the next Christmas season we were up and running.

I hope after reading this, you've gotten ideas as to how it's possible to have your very own studio. You CAN do it yourself and accomplish it without breaking the bank! Of course, everyone's situation is different-you may need to add more in the budget for additional backdrops, or you already have a lighting kit. Either way, the total budget for this project will reflect your needs. So, my estimates should ronly be considered as guidance, not the rule. Hopefully after reading this, you have found some useful information to help cut down on your cost for a small home studio. Take time to consider what is essential for you to purchase now and what could be added later.

Approximate studio cost: $558.00 without camera.

Three Point Lighting

Three Point Lighting
Basic Photography Lighting Setup for Studio
3-Point Lighting

Three-point lighting is a standard method used in visual media such as theater, video, film, still photography and computer-generated imagery. A photographer normally uses three separate positions to control the shading and shadows produced by direct lighting.

The *key light* shines directly upon the subject and serves as its principal illuminator; more than anything else, the strength, color and angle of the key determines the shot's overall lighting design.

The *fill light* also shines on the subject, but from a side angle relative to the key light and is often placed at a lower position than the key light by either lessening or eliminating chiaroscuro effects on the subject or helps control the shadow cast by a person's nose upon the rest of the face.

The *backlight* shines on the subject from behind, often to one side or the other. It gives the subject a rim of light, serving to separate the subject from the background and highlighting contours.

A high-end lighting kit such as used by professional photographers can run as much as $3,000. To cut back on costs, look for sales on essential equipment if you opt to do a home studio or consider renting equipment for the season to see what works best for your business.

Traditional Santa Photography Poses

The child or children by themselves
Santa behind them
Santa sitting next to them
Sitting on Santa's lap
The magical shots of standing next to Santa or at his feet

How to Hold a Baby

As Santa, you will have the opportunity to hold a mom's precious child in your arms. You must remember that you need to make certain that you have taken the proper precautions on ensuring the safety of the newborn. The following describes how to appropriately prepare for newborn photos and the preferred holding positions of the children for photos.

How to prepare for photos with a newborn:

1. Clean Hands – Always ensure you have washed your hands prior to putting your gloves and holding the child.

2. Clean White Gloves – Always ensure your gloves are clean. The gloves hide hangnails, hand imperfections, jewelry, tattoos, etc.

3. Make Yourself Comfortable – Always allow the parent(s) to place the child in your arms. Never reach for the baby.

4. Offer Support – Always ensure that you support the child's neck. Babies have very little neck control. *Caution:* Try to ensure that you do not press of the soft spots on the top of baby's head, also known as "fontanelles".

5. Safety First – In an ideal world, when doing photography, it is always best to have someone be a spotter for the baby. Babies need to be supervised by a responsible adult at all times. *Remember: No baby portrait with Santa is worth jeopardizing the safety of the client.*

These tips will help you avoid discomfort for the baby:

1. The baby's head should always be free, while supporting an infant's neck, so that he/she can turn around to breathe.

2. If you are nervous holding the baby, you can choose a sitting position that will help you support the baby's weight comfortably.

3. Do not show your negative emotions, such as frustration, when you are holding the baby, as you might accidentally shake the baby which can have serious repercussions.

4. Let the parents wake the child up by touching his/her cheeks or tickle her feet gently.

ALWAYS – Baby is the last child to be put in place for the photo. Always ask the parent to place the baby in your arms. So, if there are multiple children in the photo, arrange for the older child(ren) to be placed first and then the parent can place the baby in your arms.

Baby Holding Positions

1. Shoulder hold:

— This is one of the most natural holds for a newborn. With the baby's body parallel to yours, lift the baby to your shoulder height.

— Rest the baby's head on your shoulder so that she can look behind you.

— Support the baby's head and neck with one hand, and the bottom with another hand.

— This position allows your baby to hear your heartbeat.

2. Cradle hold:

— Cradling is quite simple and natural.

— With the baby parallel to your chest level, slide your hand from his/her bottom up to support the head and neck.

— Gently place your baby's head into the crook of your elbow.

— Now move your hand from the neck to the bottom and hips.

— Bring your baby close to you, and you can quickly bring the baby to sleep.

3. Belly hold:

— Lay the baby with stomach facing down on one of your forearms with head up over the elbow.

— Let the baby's feet land on either side of your hand, at an angle closer to the ground level.

— Lay your other hand across the baby's back to make him/her feel secure and to ensure the safety of the little one.

Photography with a screaming toddler

Personal note: I had a Santa tell me one time that if you are having problems with a toddler, use the "Bait and Switch" technique. The parents walk the child up and sit with him or her next to Santa. Next thing you know if the photographer, parent, and Santa have a pre-arranged sign, the parents will walk the child (back facing you), put the child on your lap and back away. Be prepared for a crying photo shot. Consider that you may be unable to calm the child, but the parent still wants the shot, so be ready for the photographer to snap the photo quickly. Then Santa needs to ensure that he safely hands the child back to the parent. Photographers have used this technique for years.

Paws with Claus

"Paws with Claus" is an ever-popular event for the special children of the family, but in my opinion, it is truly for the parents of these children. Please ensure when you are contracting with any merchant that you have an understanding both verbally and written about this event. According to my veterinarian, most animals perceive the gloves as a set of claws, so be careful when you first interact with the animal.

Quick tips:

— Pets should always be considered as children and should be treated as such.

— Ensure that you take any necessary medications for allergies or hay fever before working with pets.

— Always invite the "Parent/Owner" to be part of the photo. This will reduce the stress that the pet incurs during the photo session.

— Always ask the photographer to have a clean-up crew standing by to clean up any "accidents."

— Also keep some form of cloth with a waterproof backing to put on your lap, so the animal does not ruin your suit.

Please Note: One of the biggest things to remember: You will encounter human clients who are allergic to pet hair, pet odors, pet saliva, or dandruff. It is your responsibility to ensure that you do not conduct a "Paws with Claus" event and then see human clients without first changing out your entire suit and ensuring you wash your hands and face.

— Suggested items for this event:
— Dog Whistle
— Extra Gloves
— Place a dry pad under your suit in case of accidents.

Mini Session

So, the question always comes up: what is a mini session in the photography world? The simple answer - the name says it all. It is a truly short session with a client and a photographer that usually takes no longer than 30 minutes and snaps at least 100 photos. Usually, a photographer only does these photo sessions pre-booked in order to keep the families moving steadily through the sessions. Both Santas and photographers consider mini sessions to be quick and easy money depending on how much work is required after the session. This event is extremely popular with photographers who do not own their own studio.

As a Santa, always ask the photographer what he or she expects and how long the full session will run. Santa is "a prop" for the photographer and it is your responsibility to follow their lead. Always smile and engage with the child and always focus on the children. Make sure you give ample time for the photographer to get photos of you talking with the children and photos of all of you smiling at the camera.

Ask the photographer in advance if you can leave your business card behind for the clients. Clarify who is expected to bring candy canes, props, and any other items with you.

Depending on your interest, budget, time, experience, and available room in your home, you may opt to pursue creating an in-home photography studio. However, this may be a long-term process. You might do better to develop a solid professional relationship with a local photographer who already has access to the equipment and would enjoy being Santa's photographer at events and visits. Collaborating with an established photographer who knows how to manage children is a major asset to having satisfied clients and developing repeat clients and great referrals for new clients. Consider how much time, stress, and money it could save your Santa business to have a professional photographer partnering with you.

Concluding Thoughts

Technology provides a new and innovative platform but does come at the cost of time and effort to develop the skills needed to effectively use the technology and the financial cost to acquire and maintain the equipment. Consider the various benefits such as being able to create fun videos for social media and websites, connecting through teleconference calls/Zoom™ and photo sessions with families and pets. All of these help create special memories for your clients to reminisce fondly as time marches forward and children grow up. Then take a moment to think realistically about your business budget and plan to research and incorporate the necessary technical equipment over time. Remember to enjoy engaging with your clients, whether in person or through virtual means, and the magic Santa brings wherever and however he spends time with clients, especially the children!

Chapter 5

Non-verbal Communications

I'm dreaming of a white Christmas, just like the ones I used to know.
— Irving Berlin

Understanding Facial Expressions

As Santas, while we are enjoy being jolly, we need to learn how to read clients' facial expressions. Learning how to read facial expressions will help you understand your clients. Recognizing their level of excitement, comfort, and potential anxiety, will make your visit the best it can be.

First, you must understand the face and its expressions, also known as micro expressions. These micro expressions can inform us what someone is feeling. As Santa, most of our clients are under the age of ten, which makes our job of reading facial expressions a tad easier. We must remember that our job as Santa is to help the individual feel safe when he/she is interacting with us.

Sometimes a child may be nervous about visiting with Santa. This may be obvious with the child's demeanor and behavior or may be recognized by noticing micro expressions. To change the situation with the child, interact with the parent/guardian/caretaker by just having an idle chat discussion about when he/she was a child and how much fun it was to sit and talk to Santa.

How to Read a Face

Knowing how to read and interpret micro expressions is an essential part of understanding nonverbal behavior and reading your clients. This will play a vital role in determining the way you interact with each child.

The medical community agrees that a micro expression is an involuntary facial display that happens with 1/25th of a second. The display of facial movement is difficult for someone to conceal or change as it reflects what the person is feeling at that moment.

To understand micro expressions, you need to know there are traditional seven universal expressions: contempt, surprise, fear, happiness, sadness, anger, and disgust.

The 7 Micro Expressions

1) *"Surprise Micro expressions"* include:
- Raised and curved eyebrows.
- Below the brow the skin is stretched.
- Horizontal wrinkles on the forehead.
- You can see the whites of the eye showing above and below.
- There is no tension or stretching of the mouth and the jaw drops open.
  and drawn back or the lips are slightly tensed.

2) **_"Fear Micro expressions"_** include:
   – Normally the eyebrows are in a flat line but raised and drawn together.
   – You will notice wrinkles only on the forehead only between the eyebrows.
   – You will notice the upper eyelid is normally raised while the lower eyelid is drawn-up and tense.
   – Normally the upper whites of the eyes are showing.
   – In addition, the mouth is generally opened while the lips are either stretched

3) **_"Disgust Micro expressions"_** include:
   – Raised upper eyelid
   – Your lower lip is raised
   – A wrinkled nose
   – Raised cheeks
   – There are lines under your lower eyelid
   Easiest way to remember this one – Just think of smelling something bad.

4) **_"Anger Micro expressions"_** include:
   – The eyebrows are lowered and drawn together
   – Vertical lines appear between the eyebrows
   – Lower eyelids are tensed
   – Eyes are in hard stare or bulging
   – The lips are firmly pressed together.
   – Dilated nostrils.
   – The lower part of the jaw juts out
   Most of the facial areas do not show any ambiguity.

5) **_"Happiness Micro expressions"_** include:
   – The lips corners may be drawn back and up.
   – Mouth may not be parted, teeth exposed
   – A wrinkle runs from outer nose to outer lip
   – Cheeks are normally raised
   – The lower eyelids may show wrinkles or be tenseness.
   – Crow's feet near the outside of the eyes

6) **_"Sadness Micro expressions"_** include:
   – Inner corners of the eyebrows are drawn in and then up
   – Skin below the eyebrows is triangulated, with inner corner up
   – Corner of the lips are drawn down
   – Jaw comes up
   – Lower lip pouts out
   Just remember this is the hardest micro expression to fake!

7) *"Contempt / Hate Micro expressions"* include:
  – One side of the mouth is raised

To learn to recognize these micro expressions quickly, try practicing these emotions on yourself in front of a mirror. Another place to practice is with your friends and family. Bear this in mind – your clients will also notice your own micro expressions. Here are some additional resources on micro expressions (which may be useful but are not endorsed):

https://en.wikipedia.org/wiki/Microexpression
https://www.youtube.com/watch?v=rGhOuA3rr1k
https://www.scienceofpeople.com/microexpressions/

Understanding Body Language

Santa's body language is "always under examination" by both children and adults. Children notice your body language quicker than anything else. If Santa enters a room with high energy, the children will be excited; and vice versa, if Santa enters the room with low energy, the room will be humdrum with energy. A simple way to think about your Santa visit: You are the light bulb in the room. It's your job to light up the room with laughter. Remember to leave the room with high energy and high anticipation of your next visit.

In order to make that happen, we are going to take some time to discuss the non-verbal language which Santa emits to his clients and what the clients are telling Santa without telling Santa. As Santa, we need to learn our non-verbal language as well as the non-verbal language of our clients. Too many times, we become frustrated or discouraged when we cannot get the shy child to "hello" to Santa.

Eye Contact
As Santa, you should always make eye contact with everyone in the room. When the child or the adult is sitting on your lap, you as Santa, you need to focus your attention on that child. However, please understand that too much eye contact could be considered a sign of aggression. The best advice is to look at someone for a second or two when you first make contact.

Leaning Back
Leaning back with your arms out and your legs out in front of you signals that you are just not interested in this conversation. Instead, to show interest, sit straight up or lean in towards the person.

Crossed Arms and/or Legs

As Santa, we need to ensure that we keep our arm and legs from becoming crossed. Experts have indicated that this type of body language is on the defensive side, like someone disagreeing with your opinions or actions with whom you are interacting. In a one-on-one meeting it is recommended that when someone leans back with their arms crossed, that it is time to end the discussion.

Clasped Hands

The easiest way to describe this, you are holding your own hand. This activity does not project self-assurance. Rather, it signals nervousness which can impact your visit with the child by making the child feel nervous as well.

Hands Behind Back or In Pockets

Many children when they approach Santa, use this natural position unconsciously. Many of us consider hands in the pockets as a sign of something to hide. Or this could indicate feelings of awkwardness; unsure of how to act in front of someone.

Nodding your Head

As adults, we all do this – nod our head. We consider this to be a natural normal activity of active communication that lets others know that you are listening. Nodding your head too much however loses its effect. It is okay to nodding your head as a child gives you his/her list. As a solution, tilting your head shows that you are listening keenly. If you need to, you can always look away and come back to the person.

Touching Your Face

Touching your face, especially your nose and mouth, is another one of those gestures that is unconsciously interpreted as a sign of deception — or resistance, if you are listening rather than speaking.

Stroking Your Beard

When you are visiting with children, what happens if you stroke your beard, and a child asks you why you are doing this? Here is one way to answer: "I am deep in thought about your question or request." This body gesture usually occurs when someone is trying to come to a decision.

Tapping Your Fingers

Santa, please remember that tapping or drumming the fingers is considered rude since this usually demonstrates that you are impatient or tired of waiting.

Hunching Your Shoulders

Santas, remember that when you enter a room you need to exude authority and Christmas spirit. Having hunched or slumped shoulders is seen as a sign of unhappiness. Santa needs to project happiness and confidence, stand up straight, shoulders back, and with walking at a brisk stride, like mom nagged you to do.

Glancing at a Watch or Phone

As Santa, we do need to maintain a time schedule when we are visiting our clients. This is where a Santa's helper comes into play, keeping track of the time. If Santa needs to do it himself, find a small timer to set and put it in your pocket, to avoid having to look at your watch or phone. Santa needs to pay attention to the million conversations that are going on at once. We think we can peek at the time or a text without people noticing, but they always do.

Santa Claus Expectations When Dealing with Children and Families

Santa visits children and adults as a symbol of love, peace, and kindness. Santa is supposed to be a jolly, cheery, gentle, and non-judgmental character.

Santa should NEVER step out of character. At no time Santa should make any comments which are negative or derogatory. It is also not his place to discipline anyone. Santa's comments should be jolly or gentle, but most of all caring.

Based on years of Santa experience, these are the *"CLEAR BEST"* things to remember about what to say and do while visiting with the children.

1. C: Always *Compliment*
2. L: Tell the Children you *Love* Them
3. E: *Encourage* the Children to say Something
4. A: *Adapt* to the Needs of the Children
5. R: Show a *Real* Interest

6. B: **Be** Engaging with the Child
7. E: **Engage** with Others as Well:
8. S: **Special** Needs Children
9. T: **Thank** the Children for Coming

1. C: Always Compliment

I have always tried to find something nice to say about the child's name, attire, hair, hair decorations or patience while waiting in line. Make children feel that they are valued. Make the child proud of their accomplishments. Ask the parents to remind you about key items or events for which the child should get credit/praise.

2. L: Tell the Children you Love Them

Many children grew up in a household where love was not always expressed verbally. For any child, it is important to hear words of affirmation. Tell the child, "It's great to see you again," or "I'm so glad you came to see me today." Let them know that on Christmas Eve you will check in on them. Make the child feel special.

3. E: Encourage the Children to say Something

Always take the time to encourage the children to talk. Ask the child who is here with them such as siblings, parents, and grandparents. If the siblings are smaller or upset, ask the oldest what their siblings would like for Christmas. You also can ask who will be with them for Christmas.

4. A: Adapt to the Needs of the Children

Sometimes children lose their thought process when they reach the big chair. Always "Go with the flow" of the child: Let them make the first move and let them speak. Ask one question at a time, then give them time to answer.

5. R: Show a Real Interest

One of the best subjects to discuss with a child is their accomplishments in school. Inquire about which grade the child is in? Favorite subject? Favorite activity? Favorite sport? And most of all, WHY is it their favorite? Elf on the Shelf is a big subject this time of the year. Also, be sure to include their pets in the discussion.

6. B: Be Engaging with the Child

Every Santa has a different twist on how he portrays Santa in diverse environments. Don't be glued to your chair! Getting up out the chair and taking the time to talk to a child in line breaks the ice for everyone waiting to reach the "big chair." If a child does not want to come to Santa, go to the child. Sit on the floor become engaged in the activity he or she is doing.

7. E: Engage with Others as Well

Of course you will ask if the child has been good. Ask for confirmation – "What would [name] say? Carefully chat or joke with teenage siblings and adults about when they once sat on your knee. If the child says he/she has been bad, remind the child that unruly behavior does not mean he/she is a bad child. Good people make poor decisions, but that does not make them bad people.

8. S: Special Needs Children

Special needs can be mental, physical, emotional or a combination of all of these. Santa Claus takes particular care in responding to each individual's needs – no exception! For a special needs child, the extra love and time you spend with them means a lot to families who might not otherwise be able to make it through a visit with Santa.

9. T: Thank the Children

The best for last. ALWAYS thank the children for coming. Give the children a high-five. Do it! Younger children like to fist bump. Always tell the parents you have wonderful children - what parent doesn't love to hear that? Be careful with hugs -never initiate a hug with a child, instead, let the child give you a hug if they wish.

Concluding Thoughts

Santa needs to be able to discern what a child is feeling through nonverbal body language and facial expressions. This knowledge allows Santa to respond in such a way that the child can relax, be at ease and feel safe. When the child is comfortable, then the Santa visit will be both enjoyable and memorable in positive ways. Learn to recognize when a child is nervous: Give the child space and time to process what is happening, speak quietly and calmly, and always let the child know how much you appreciate the visit. Adapt to the child's needs, support the child, and encourage the child to understand that Santa believes every child is good and special. As you gain experience, these things will come quickly and naturally. If you are unsure of how to respond in any situation, just remember "CLEAR BEST"!

Chapter 6

Reporting Child Abuse

Christmas is doing a little something extra for someone.
— Charles M. Schulz

Reporting Child Abuse

What should you do if you encounter a child and suspect that they are a victim of child abuse? If possible, obtain the child's name and address and assure them that they are on your "Good List." Take note of any evidence of physical or other abuse – suggest a free "photo with Santa" to do so. Keep calm and be reassuring during your visit with the child. Let the child know that teachers, doctors, and police officers are Santa's good friends, and they can help the child. As soon as you can after the visit, call the police or other authority to pass along your concerns and any evidence you collected. The authorities will check and investigate as needed to be sure the child is safe.

Who is a Mandatory Reporter of Child Abuse?

All states require that certain defined persons (such as pediatricians, teachers, and childcare workers) who know or suspect that child abuse is occurring must report the abuse to the authorities. These mandatory reporting laws were instituted to help promote awareness of child abuse and early intervention, if possible. As such, the laws make reporting quite straightforward.

There is no reason to be hesitant about making a report if you genuinely suspect that child abuse is occurring. The reporting laws generally do not punish people for making a good faith effort to report child abuse, if after investigation the claim turns out to be unfounded. In most states, reports can be anonymous. You may be the one person who can protect this child from any future harm.

Contrast this with a child abuse report that is not based on good faith. A person who reports child abuse without any basis for such a belief and motivated entirely by a desire to get a reported person in trouble with the law, is guilty of malice.

Are You a Mandatory Reporter of Child Abuse?

In at least 18 states, anyone and everyone who knows or suspects that child abuse has occurred is required by law to make a report. In most states, professions that engage in regular contact with children are normally listed as mandatory reporters.

Each state maintains its own laws and regulations designating the groups of professionals who are required to report cases of suspected child abuse and neglect.

It is your responsibility to check with your state to find out what you are legally required to do.

Check with your state or local authorities.

Physical Contact with Clients

As Santa, we often hold, hug or otherwise touch our clients during visits. We must be certain that we do not accidentally wind up placing our hands in awkward spots, hug too snugly or even pat a shoulder, if it makes our clients feel uncomfortable. We must always be diligent in ensuring that our clients feel safe in our presence. Also, during any visit or event, do not allow yourself to be alone with one single child. Always remember the *Rule of 3:* Both you and the child are protected by having a third party with you.

There are three things to remember:

— Always wear your gloves
— Clearly show where your hands are at all times
— Never put yourself in a compromising position

Safe touches. These are touches that keep children safe and are good for them, and that make children feel cared for and important. Safe touches can include hugging, pats on the back or an arm around the shoulder. Safe touches are touches made in an appropriate manner with the child and parent's consent.

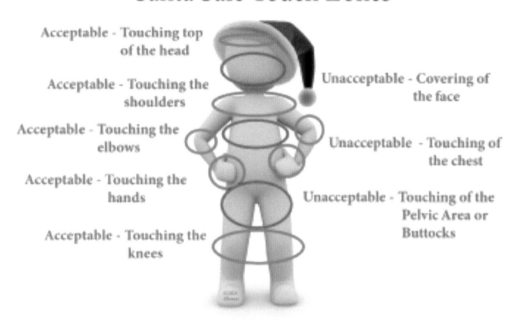

DISCLAIMER: This is a general guide. Santas should alaways ask the parents and child before touching.This graphic does not take in consideration for religious and or cultural practices. Santas should ensure that any touching should be visible with the white gloves.

Remember these are the **"NO GO"** rules

It is *NEVER* okay to touch someone else's private body parts.

It is *NEVER* okay to touch your own private body parts in front of anyone.

It is *NEVER* okay for someone to ask you to touch his or her private body parts.

It is *NEVER* okay take your clothes off or to take pictures or videos of you with your clothes off.

It is *NEVER* okay for someone to show you photos or videos of people without their clothes on.

It is *NEVER* okay to do unsafe touches. These are touches that hurt children's bodies or feelings (For example: hitting, pushing, pinching, and kicking or unwanted touches anywhere, anytime).

109

Concluding Thoughts

In the world today, it is absolutely awful and horrifying to know that some children are mistreated and abused. Being a Santa is a heavy responsibility in some ways, but simultaneously a joy in recognizing that you can provide a safe and fun experience for children. Protecting both yourself and your clients is of utmost importance, but so is having a happy and enjoyable Christmas moment for you both. Learn to recognize when a child/client is nervous, how to put them at ease and keep them safe. Consider how much this visit/event means to your clients and know that you have done your best to make that experience memorable for all involved.

Chapter 7

Santa's Suit

"God put Santa Claus on earth to remind us that Christmas is 'sposed to be a happy time."
— Bil Keane

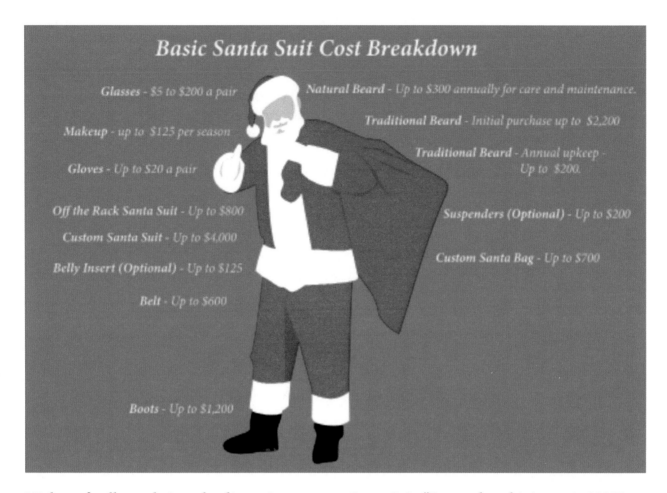

Basic Santa Suit Cost Breakdown

Glasses - $5 to $200 a pair

Makeup - up to $125 per season

Gloves - Up to $20 a pair

Off the Rack Santa Suit - Up to $800

Custom Santa Suit - Up to $4,000

Belly Insert (Optional) - Up to $125

Belt - Up to $600

Boots - Up to $1,200

Natural Beard - Up to $300 annually for care and maintenance.

Traditional Beard - Initial purchase up to $2,200

Traditional Beard - Annual upkeep - Up to $200.

Suspenders (Optional) - Up to $200

Custom Santa Bag - Up to $700

We have finally made it to the discussion on your Santa Suit. "Remember this is a suit, **NOT** a costume." Once you don the suit you become Santa: Anyone who sees you will recognize and treat you as the Santa of books and legends. For this reason, many Santas consider having a custom-made suit to be a required and essential part of being Santa. However, most of the Santas working today use off-the-rack suits with no issues.

Personal Note: Sitting in meetings or trainings I have heard professional Santas say they started out with an off-the-rack suit. Honestly, having a custom-made suit changes nothing for you except your appearance. You are the same Santa you were before with only one exception; your self-confidence level went up. Honestly, truth be told, I have used a $60 off the rack Santa suit from Rubies (Amazon) for the past 6 years. Everyone has loved the suit. I prefer them over the custom-made suit. The only issue with the suit was that it needed another belt loop.

During this section, we will be discussing the items that make Santa look and feel authentic.

The Evolution of Santa's Suit

If you remember back in the beginning of this book when we discussed the origins of Santa Claus, you probably realized that the Santa you portray today has been influenced and blended by many cultures.

You have probably wondered how Saint Nicholas actually dressed during his life. According to ancient customs and traditions, he probably wore an Alb, long Tunic, or Cassock, Surplice, Stole, Cape, Miter and probably carried a Crozier as part of the traditional bishop clothing of that time period, in the warm and arid climate of Turkey. The origins of our modern-day Santa Suit come from various customs and traditions molded into one current practice. However, one thing is true - "the suit" reminds us of Christian beliefs and heritage.

A brief example is that the color of the Santa Suit comes from the red of the bishop's robe or the blood that Jesus Christ shed on the cross. The white in the fur represents forgiveness (purity) for all sins. The candy cane comes from the bishop's staff and can be read as a "J" for Jesus or as a staff. This section will dig deeper into the reason why the suit is the way it is today, helping to understand the religious implications of our suit.

As the legend of Saint Nicholas evolved throughout Europe, his clothing changed to adapt to the weather conditions in Nordic countries. Other pre-Victorian depictions show Santa Claus figures dressed in robes of various colors or in different colored suits. In northern Europe, St. Nicholas traded in his bishop's miter and crosier for a fur-trimmed red suit and fur cap.

While every region and country around the globe has its own unique version of Santa, this book will focus on the evolution of the original Santa/St. Nicholas into the modern Santa known and loved in the United States of America. The best way to describe how Santa Claus is now dressed is to say he had a wardrobe makeover during the 1800s, presented in now-famous American literature.

According to *'Twas the Night Before Christmas*, the poem describes St. Nicholas being warm, friendly, and pleasantly plump while wearing a tan suit. In the time period between Livingston's poem and Thomas Nast, Santa Claus appearance varied in many ways. For instance, in 1837, Robert Weir, an art teacher at West Point painted the first known American portrait of Santa Claus. In this painting, Weir depicted Santa as short, beardless man who dressed in high boots with a short coat with a stocking cap. Then in 1841, The Parkinson's Confectionery in Philadelphia displayed Santa Claus dressed in a suit that had striped pants along with stockings and a flying doublet with a tasseled cap on his heard with a pipe.

Prior to William Holbrook Beard's painting in 1862, most American artists derived their descriptions of Santa Claus from Clement Clarke Moore's 1823 poem *A Visit from Saint Nicholas*. In his 1862 painting *Santa Claus*, Beard depicted Santa Claus in a residential area urban landscape, riding above rooftops in a sky clouded by coal smoke. He pilots a delicate swan boatdrawn by reindeer whose harnesses are decorated with silver bells.

Santa Claus, ca. 1862 painted by William Holbrook Beard. Courtesy of the Rhode Island School of DesignMuseum, Providence, RI.

Thomas Nast, a political cartoonist, originally standardized Santa Claus image during the Civil War and continued refining the Santa Claus image until 1886. It has been long believed that Nast used himself as the model for the jolly elf. Nast created the covers of *Harper's Weekly* with a Santa who looked like a gnome or elf, wearing fur-trimmed red suits, instead of the original tan suit color. In addition, the image of a white-bearded, red suited man was used in advertising campaigns including for the US Confection Company's Sugar Plums and on the cover of humor magazine *Puck*.

Taylor, C. J. (1896) Puck Christmas/ C.J. Taylor. , 1896. N.Y.: Published by Keppler & Schwarzmann, December 9. [Photograph] Retrieved from the Library of Congress, https://www.loc.gov/item/2012648493/.

As the legend of Saint Nicholas evolved throughout Europe, his clothing changed to adapt to the weather conditions in Nordic countries. Other pre-Victorian depictions show Santa Claus figures dressed in robes of various colors or in different colored suits. In northern Europe, Saint Nicholas traded in his bishop's miter and crosier for a fur-trimmed red suit and fur cap.

In December of 1913, Norman Rockwell took up where Nast stopped. He drew an illustration of Santa for the cover of the *Boys Life* magazine with a red fur-trimmed suit and hat with cheery checks. Rockwell was known for drawing Santa in his toy workshop while wearing an apron.

In the 1920s, J.C. Leyendecker changed the look of Santa Claus; a man both jolly and round, with a noticeably ruddy complexion, dressed in a red suit (white trim included), a red cap, and the signature belt and boots. He was able to create a universal Kris Kringle style. As Leyendecker continued to present this new look on the covers of The *Saturday Evening Post* and other notable magazines, the public openly accepted this new image of Saint Nick.

Arguably, Leyendecker's biggest success was in 1931 with the Coca-Cola™ Company's Christmas advertisement campaign. This campaign led most Americans to associate Coca-Cola™ as the creators of the Santa we know and love today. The Swedish American illustrator, Haddon Sundblom, hired by Coca-Cola™ to create this Christmas advertisement, received the credit for Santa's red and white suit, even though it was Thomas Nast who is generally credited with the color change over 40 years earlier. What is not commonly known is that in 1875, Louis Prang printed a series of the first Christmas cards picturing Santa in a red suit.[23] However, while many attributed today's image of Santa Claus to Sundblom, what they do not realize is that artist Fred Mizen drew Santa drinking a Coke™ at the Famous Barr Co., in St. Louis, Missouri, a year prior.

Biblical Meaning Behind Santa's Outfit

Each piece of St. Nicholas' outfit represented a particular element of the clothing worn by the bishops of the Catholic or Orthodox Church. These items were special symbols taken directly from the Christian Bible and served as reminders to church members. Later on, Santa became less of a religious representation of Christmas, instead, seen by the public as a secular part of the Christmas holiday season.

Listed below are the rituals, definitions, and the meanings of the vestments that a bishop would wear as part of their normal outfit:

As a bishop would start dressing into his vestments, it is required that the bishop washes his hands while reciting the appropriate prayer. This is complete symbolism, as being wash of your sin before entering the sanctuary of the Most High. Catholics cite Exodus 3:5, being the symbolic equivalent of removing the sandals before the burning bush. [24]

> **Prayer:** *"Da, Domine, virtutem manibus meis ad abstergendam omnem maculam; ut sine pollutione mentis et corporis valeam tibi servire"* (Give virtue to my hands, O Lord, that being cleansed from all stain I might serve you with purity of mind and body)."

Amice – a rectangular neck cloth that is used to protect the chasuble and stole. According to the Catholic Church, the amice symbolic as "the helmet of salvation." [25] The helmet is supposed to protect those who wear it from evil thoughts and desires during liturgical celebration.

116

Prayer: *"Impone, Domine, capiti meo galeam salutis, ad expugnandos diabolicos incursus" (Place upon me, O Lord, the helmet of salvation, that I may overcome the assaults of the devil)."*

Alb – a long white linen tunic-like robe worn under the chasuble, worn over the priest's clothes. The name alb comes from the Latin word alba, meaning "white". The white of the alb is a symbol of purity and freedom from sin. Purity is required to enter the Kingdom of Heaven. [26] It represents the white robe with which Herod clothed Jesus in when he sent Him back to Pilate. This is the prayer the priest says while putting on the alb:

Prayer - *"Cleanse me, O Lord, and purify my heart; that being made white in the Blood of the Lamb, I may come to eternal joy."*

Cassock – a floor length garment with 33 buttons representing Christ 33 years on the earth and five buttons on each sleeve symbolizing the five wounds of Christ.

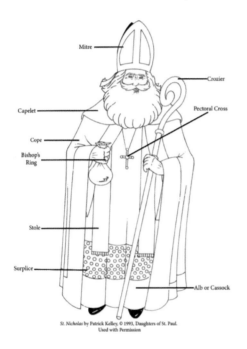

St. Nicholas by Patrick Kelley, © 1993, Daughters of St. Paul. Used with Permission

Chasuble – a liturgical sleeveless vestment that is worn for celebrating mass. The color changes with the liturgical year and special events. It is the final vestment of a priest that is worn on top of all the other clothing. This symbolizes the virtue of charity and yoke of unselfish love. This piece of clothing refers to Colossians 3:14.

Prayer – *O Lord, who has said, My yoke is easy and My burden is light; grant that I may be able so to bear it, that I may obtain Thy grace. Amen*

Cincture – a cord used as a belt to tighten the alb symbolizing the virtue of chastity and continence. The cincture is normally the same color as the chasuble. The cincture represents the Fruits of the Spirit which are found in Galatians 5:22.

Prayer – *"Praecinge me, Domine, cingulo puritatis, et exstingue in lumbis meis humorem libidinis; ut maneat in me virtus continentiae et cas titatis" (Gird me, O Lord, with the cincture of purity, and quench in my heart the fire of concupiscence, that the virtue of continence and chastity may abide in me).*

Collare – a white collar that looks like a short bib that is worn under the cassock. The material matches the color of the cassock.

Crozier — In the Western religion, the Crozier, or officially the pastoral staff (baculus pastoralis), symbolizes the role of bishop as the Good Shepherd. According to the Gospel of St. John 10:1-21, Jesus identified Himself as the Good Shepherd. The word in the original Greek text is kalos, which means "good" or "model." The bishop, like a good shepherd, must lead his faithful flock along the path of salvation, disciplining and protecting them as needed. The shepherd's staff is therefore a most appropriate symbol for the office of bishop.

In the Eastern religion, the two snakes found on the Crozier represent the time when Moses led the Israelites out of Egypt and the Israelites were suffering from snake bites due to speaking out against God. When the people repented, God directed Moses to fashion an image of brass and have those who were sick look upon it and be healed, according to Numbers 21:8.

Dalmatic and Tunicle — never worn by priests, as priests, but both are worn by bishops under the chasuble (never under the cope). These may also be worn prelates (who are not bishops) to whom the pope has conceded the right to wear the episcopal vestments. The tunicle is a shorter version of the dalmatic and worn by subdeacons.

Mitre — a symbol of intelligence and wisdom. The mitre is a "headdress", worn for liturgical functions as is the crozier and pallium. The word mitre comes from the Greek mitra, which signifies a headband or diadem. In the Old Testament, the High Priest and other priests wore a distinctive garb which included a mitre. The church refers to Exodus 39:27-31 and Leviticus 8:7-9 to explain why a mitre is used in the modern church. In the Eastern religion, the Miter looks like more of a crown because in the days of Emperor Constantine bishops had great authority. In the Western religion, the Miter represents the Tongues of Fire which fell on the heads of the apostles at Pentecost. The ribbon on the left side of the Miter represents the Old Testament and the right-side ribbon represents the New Testament which signifies when the word became flesh.

Pectoral Cross — worn by the Holy Father, cardinals, bishops, and abbots. The word pectoral derives from the Latin pectus, meaning "breast." This cross is attached to a chain and is worn on the chest, near the heart. When putting on the pectoral cross, traditionally the bishop says, "Munire me digneris," asking the Lord for strength and protection against all evil and all enemies, and to be mindful of His passion and cross.

Stole — a long scarf worn by Roman magistrates when engaged in their official duties, just as modern judges wear a court gown. Whenever a priest celebrates Mass or administers the Sacraments, he wears the stole as a sign that he is occupied with an official priestly duty. When placing the stole about his neck, in vesting for Mass, the priest begs God to give him on the last day the 'garment of immortality' that was forfeited by our sinful first parents. The Catholic Church takes the authority for this piece of clothing from Numbers 15:38-39.

Prayer — *"Redde mihi, Domine, stolam immortalitatis, quam perdidi in praevaricatione primi parentis; et, quamvis indignus accedo ad tuum sacrum mysterium, merear tamen gaudium sempiternum. (Return to me, O Lord, the of immortality, which I have lost in the sin of my parent; and although I, unworthy, approach. Thy sacred mystery, grant to me, nevertheless, everlasting joy)."*

Hopefully you will now see some of the connections between the Bible and the robes worn by church bishops, as well as understand why St. Nicholas dressed as he did, being a bishop of the Church. Even now, when looking at a modern Santa suit, you can catch a glimpse of these connections and be reminded that Santa originally was deeply associated with St. Nicholas. Further on in this book, there will be more information on the secularization of Santa.

Examples of these connections:

Bells are a musical sound for us; they grab our attention. In some places, like Palestine, shepherds use bells to lead their flocks of sheep. Remember, the bishop of the church is responsible for the local church flock and bells ring to call the congregation to worship.

Santa Belt Buckle —This has replaced the Holy Cross that the bishop would wear.

Santa Hat — shaped as a triangle for symbolic purposes like the Bishop's Miter.

Santa Jacket — represents the cape that a bishop wears. In the 1800's the jacket was shortened, and fur was placed on the jacket to combine some the Nordic traditions of Christmas.

Staff — Used to symbolize the role of shepherd, protecting and disciplining the sheep. As the Santa suit evolved from St. Nicholas (a church bishop) carrying a Crozier to modern times, this staff is sometimes seen in American illustrations and is still seen as part of Santa's suit, particularly in other countries.

Modern Santa Suit Elements

Santa Belts — As a professional Santa, you need to give meticulous attention to every detail of your appearance and presentation, including your belt. The exact style, fit, cost and overall look play a vital role in your portrayal of Santa.

Santa Glasses – Santa glasses come in many shapes and designs. However, the styles that the American public associates with Santa the most are the golden rectangle glasses or the golden round glasses.

Naugahyde Belts (also called "Pirate" belts) – This belt comes with most of the off-the-rack suits. It is not recommended to use this belt unless you are extremely careful. It is made of artificial leather that is a composite knit fabric that contains expanded polyvinyl chloride (PVC) plastic coating. It is very flexible and therefore, very thin. It is easy to clean but does not hold up well to any stress on the grommets. The buckle is gold painted plastic and soon gets scratched revealing the whitish plastic underneath.

Leather Belts – If you buy a leather belt, found out how it was dyed and how it holds up under continued usage. You can purchase a belt from anywhere, starting with your local cobbler or horse tack store first. Then pursue another source, such as an online leather company or check with another Santa to find where he gets his belts. Ensure the correct width of your belt matches your suit. Must suits need belts which measure from 3.5 inches to 4.0 inches. Always measure the circumference of your "cookie zone" with your padding and suit on to ensure you have the correct measurements. Otherwise, you will have a wide belt to wear for your everyday outfits instead of for your Santa suit.

These glasses can be non-prescription costume glasses which cost as little as $5.00, which is great if you do not need prescription glasses, or if you wear contact lenses. On the other hand, if you wear prescription glasses you might consider purchasing "Santa" frames and prescription lenses, if you do not or cannot wear contacts and want to be sure you do not trip over things while you are portraying Santa. As you plan for business expenses, be sure to include the cost of this item, especially if you do get them made with prescription lenses!

Santa Gloves – The tradition of Santa wearing gloves dates back to the Coca-Cola™ Christmas advertisements, when Santa's gloves wore large leather gloves used for work, such as handling the reins of the reindeer. As for today's Santa, he is expected to wear white gloves when meeting and greeting children. The gloves need to be clean and extend past your wrist in order to cover up any scars or tattoos.

It is important that you find a distributor of white gloves also commonly known as "band gloves". Be sure to find a pair which fits you properly and ensure that the gloves cover up any tattoos. Consider purchasing nylon-polyester gloves because cotton gloves get dirty faster and require more cleaning.

Santa Belly Insert (Optional) – Since Santa comes in various sizes and dimensions, you may want to add some extra padding around the cookie zone (aka belly). A Santa belly insert allows you to instantly grow your cookie zone without putting on any weight! There are many options out on the internet. Find what works for you and your suit. Make sure you suit can accommodate any changes you decide to make. Your Santa Belly can be either pre-stuffed or self-stuffed. As a side note, being able to change your belly size allows you to more easily retain your "civilian" anonymity.

Santa Boots – Santa boots are an item that can either break you or make you with your clients. Everyone will notice cheap boots such as the shoe cover boots. This can lead to awkward questions from your younger clients and might also hinder your chances of repeat clients. You have multiple options when it comes to style and cost, but make sure you are comfortable with both standing and walking in the boots; that they are of good quality and can be cleaned/polished; and that the boots will wear well over many Christmas seasons to justify whatever money you put into this purchase.

Personal note: A Santa's choice of boots is a personal choice. I have heard of cowboy boots, firefighter boots and even steel-toed boots. There are several good boot companies that will provide you with a good boot with custom design which will cost you a pretty penny. If you happen to live near a horse tack store or a cobbler, make a visit and ask them about making you a custom boot. A good boot that will not break the bank but can last a couple of years with the proper care are the Funtasma Boots.

Santa Bags – Santa bags come in a variety of different designs, colors, and sizes. Depending on your budget you can pay $9.99 to $800 for a custom Santa bag. There are a lot of things to consider when you either order your bag or make it yourself. So, here are some items to bear in mind:

> Does your bag need to stand up on its own?
> Do you need a hidden pocket on the inside?
> Do you want a unique fabric and tassel?
> Do you need a shoulder strap?
> How many pockets do you need on or in the bag?
> Does it need to be waterproof?
> Do you need a backup bag, or one for indoor and one for outdoor events.

Gloves – As a performer, it is important that as Santa you wear white gloves since these can be easily seen in any photos. Using white gloves keeps you as Santa, protected from potential sexual misconduct lawsuits. Unfortunately, this is something you need to keep in mind as discussed earlier in this book.

Personal Note: Based upon personal experience I have found that polyester gloves cause my hands to sweat. Cotton gloves are my preference. I use wrist-long gloves with sure grips dots. The sure grips help turn pages in a book, pick up little things, help with cards, and letters.

Suspenders (Optional) – Suspenders come in two basic forms such as fabric or a combination of fabric and leather straps worn over the shoulders to hold up trousers. The suspenders may be completely elastic or only contain elastic at attachment at the clips or buttons. Suspenders are typically attached to your pant trousers with clips or buttons with leather tabs at the ends. The method of attaching the suspenders to your trousers will depend on how your pants were designed. Be sure when you buy the suspenders that your pants will support that design. Suspenders could be a great insurance policy for off-the-rack suits. Over time the elastic around the waist will fail. Suspenders help ensure that Santa suits will stay in place with no problem. Another reason to consider suspenders for your wardrobe is for when you will be expected to take off your Santa jacket for an event. Also, consider the size you will need to fit the suspenders over any chest and belly inserts.

There are Santas who will wear suspenders on the outside of their jacket which are connected to their Santa belt. ***Word of caution:*** Before spending the money ensure that your clients will support your decision to use this alternate look for Santa versus the traditional look of suspenders under the jacket.

Personal Note: Suspenders in my opinion are a must, especially the heavy-duty suspenders to help hold up your trousers on those long days.

Walking Staff (Optional) – A walking staff is a personal choice. If you need a staff in order to walk, please make your staff represent your Santa character. A personalized staff can range from a few hundred dollars to a thousand. Craft shows or outdoor sports stores can be good places to look for a walking staff.

Dry Cleaning Your Santa Suit

Taking your suit to the dry cleaners will certainly be less time consuming than hand washing. Seek out a dry cleaner that specializes in cleaning wedding dresses.

Dry cleaners with wedding dress experience tend to know exactly what chemicals will and will not work on the delicate suit materials. Also, be sure to tell the cleaner to go easy on the chemicals, since too many chemicals can cause damage. You should be reasonably safe with taking your suit to the cleaners just once a year at the end of the season before you store it.

HALCO™ provided the following recommendations for the care of their Santa suits.

> *"HALCO™ recommends that the suits must be cleaned starting with a completely clean chemical process, followed by a low heat drying temperature while using PERC chemicals."*

How to Remove Odor from Your Santa Suit

Time and time again, Santas raise the problem of having odor from their suit. So, here are a few things to think about when you are deodorizing your suit. One of the biggest items to consider is your clients. You must use a non-allergic product on your suit which does not emit an order that could trigger a respiratory issue for yourself or your client.

Here are some ideas on how to remove the smell from your suit.

1. Turn your suit inside out and lay or hang carefully over a line to air out.

2. You can mist it with some cheap Vodka and then hang or lay out to dry. The Vodka will evaporate and take most of any odor with it. It won't smell like you have been drinking all day if you do this the night before your event. Always test on your suit in a small area before spraying the entire suit.

3. My personal preference is to NOT use Dryer Sheets as the scents are too strong, and you or a child could possibly have a reaction to them at a high concentration.

4. If you have a small hand-held steamer use can use this to remove your wrinkles and sterilize your suit at the same time. When you sterilize your suit, you are removing the bacteria and other microorganisms which cause odors. *Note:* Ensure the steamer is safe for your suit prior to use.

5. Essential oil spray. A small amount of this goes a long way, but you could try something that would remind clients of the holiday season such as pine, cloves or peppermint.

In researching this segment on how to remove odors from your Santa Suit, more reasons kept popping up as to why you should *not use chemical air fresheners*. According to CV Skins study, they listed seven reasons why not to use *chemical air fresheners*.

1. Chemical air fresheners *do not remove the odor molecules* - they simply cover them up.

2. Most chemical air fresheners contain *chemicals linked to cancer.*

3. Most chemical air fresheners are linked to *hormone disruption and developmental problems.*

4. Most chemical air fresheners contain *chemicals linked to neurotoxicity,* which means the chemicals are poisonous to the nerves or nerve cells.

5. Most chemical air fresheners contain chemicals that *irritate the skin, eyes, and lungs.*

6. Most chemical air fresheners contain chemicals linked to *allergies and asthma.*

Caring for your Santa Suit Fur

Required items:

    Slicker Brush*
    Wash Cloth

Step 1 — Recommend doing at the end of each Santa shift. Lightly wipe down all the fur that can come in contact with your skin. Wiping down the fur removes the oil left from contact with your skin. The most needed places to wipe down are the collar at the back of the neck and the rim of the hat.

Step 2 — When dry, lightly brush all the fur on the Santa Suit (including the hat).

Step 3 — As required when you dry clean your suit. Lightly brush all the fur on the Santa suit (including the hat) after the suit returns home from the cleaners. Just remember if you keep the fur brushed, the fur will not become mashed, matted, and pilled.

*Slicker Brush is a pet grooming tool used on dogs and cats.

How to Clean White Fur

Required Items:

      Isopropyl Alcohol
      Distilled Water
      Dawn (Blue) dish detergent
      Fur brush

Step 1 — Gently remove any dirt which has settled on your jacket either by shaking or combing.

Step 2 — Hang your jacket up if the fur on the suit is not detachable.
Note: Never fold your jacket to clean it.

Step 3 — Brush the fur while it is hanging with a fur brush. If you do not have a brush, use your fingers.

Step 4 — If the stain remains, use a homemade cleaning solution. Mix 1-part Isopropyl Alcohol with 1 part of Distilled Water. (Some folks recommend 1 teaspoon of liquid detergent). Because the fur is delicate, always avoid any type of cleaner or solvent. Use as little of the cleaning solution as possible.

Step 5 — Rub the stain gently with a white cloth and allow to dry. Place the coat in a well-ventilated area and allow it to air dry thoroughly. The alcohol will prevent any water stains from forming on the coat or fur.

Step 6 — Repeat if necessary.

Step 7 — Brush out the fur once completely dry.

Cleaning your Santa Suit
(Without Using a Dry Cleaner)

Required Items:
        Santa Suit
        Gentle laundry detergent
        Soft cloths

Step 1 — Make a solution of cold water and laundry detergent. Go easy on the detergent to avoid leaving a soap residue behind on the fabric.

Step 2 — Spot test the detergent solution in a hidden area before you proceed.

Step 3 — Dab one cloth in the detergent solution and work a soiled spot on the suit. Start in the red colored areas and make sure not to allow the moisture to seep through or run into the white areas. Santa's suit should not have any pink areas.

Step 4 — Allow the red to dry completely before proceeding.

Step 5 — Repeat the process with a clean cloth on the white portions of the suit. (Do not use the same cloth you used to clean the red portions of the suit).

Step 6 — Allow to dry.

Step 7 — Gently brush to restore the fluff.

Restoring Leather Gloves

Required Items:
        Leather gloves
        Leather color dye set
        Cloth
        Latex-free gloves (optional – keeps dye off your hands)

Step 1 — Remove any dirt, leather creams, or protectors on the gloves with the preparer.

Step 2 —Take a cloth and wet it with the preparer. Lightly rub the glove in a circular motion with the sponge until the whole glove has been covered with the preparer.

Step 3 — After treating the gloves, wait 10 minutes for each glove to dry.

Step 4 — Stir the bottom of the bottle. DO NOT shake the bottle. Shaking the bottle creates air bubbles in the dye which thins out the application on the glove.

Step 5 — When applying the application, place the glove on the opposite hand. Gently, evenly brush the leather dye on all the surfaces of the glove.

Step 6 — Once the glove is dry, apply the 2nd coat.

Step 7 — Place glove in an upright position to dry. Let gloves dry for 6 hours in a warm, dry location. Place on 20-ounce soda bottle.

Step 8 — Use steps 1 – 7 for second glove

Companies that provide the needed products:
Tarrago
Leather Magic
Rub N Restore
TRG

Note: For Santa boots – Keep them cleaned and buffed with light boot polish and clean cloths. If you opt for non-leather footwear, do what you need to do to keep them looking clean and presentable for photographs.

How to Store Your Santa Suit

Storing your Santa suit is important to make certain that when you are ready to pull it out for your next event, it is suitable for use right away. Air circulation is essential in making certain that the suit stays smelling great and looking good too. Make sure all items are stored in a cool, dry area with plenty of room to avoid wrinkles.

— Ensure you use a padded suit hanger to hang the suit jackets. Ensure you zip the jacket up.

— Use a skirt hanger to hang your pants in order to reduce wrinkles and increase air circulation.

— Keep the suit in a cool, dark storage closet that has air circulation. Keeping the suit out of the sun reduces the fading of the velvet.

— Never fold your belt. Hang your belt on a hanger in the closet and let it dangle. This avoids creases in the belt.

— Store hat, boot covers, gloves, and other small miscellaneous items in a box with the lid off.

Remember - Air circulation is important for all pieces of your Santa suit.

Creating Your Own Santa Suit

For those who would prefer to make their own Santa suit, we have provided the following information for you. Keep in mind that if you do not have experience with sewing clothes, you will either want to practice first or hire someone to do this for you. If you choose to do your own sewing, but lack confidence with your experience or ability, then practice first on inexpensive muslin/cotton material and then try sewing on small scrap pieces of the actual fabrics you intend to use to familiarize yourself with how much you need to pin the pieces together to keep the fabric edges steady as you sew seams, as well as avoiding stretching the fabric which can cause problems.

Most fabric stores carry patterns to make outfits, the most traditional patterns are **McCall's M5550** Santa Claus Christmas Costume Sewing Pattern and **Simplicity Pattern 2542** Adult Costumes. Both patterns will need slight alterations to fit your particular needs. Watch fabric stores for sales so you can purchase materials and patterns for discounted prices. Also consider that sewing the various parts of the suit could easily take a month or more, with cutting, piecing, fitting/tweaking and finishing touches. Always start earlier than you think with sewing to allow for problems with your machine, mistakes, fittings and only having so much time to work on this project! You do not want to be stressed going into the Christmas season!

Santa Suit Jacket (Extra Large) & Hat

Item	Length of Fabric
Santa Fabric Velvet	6.0 yards
Santa Fur No Front	1.25 yards
Santa Fur Front	1.5 yards
Santa Fur Cap	2.0 yards
Lining	6.0 yards

Check-off List for Jacket

☐ Side Pockets - Left or Right or Both
☐ Inside Jacket Pocket
☐ Buttons - provided/not provided - decide your your design
☐ Chest size
☐ Sweep size
☐ Sleeve size
☐ Neck size
☐ Belly insert - measurement
☐ Width of fur
☐ Fur - decide removable or non-removable

Check off list for Santa Hat

☐ Width of fur on the Hat
☐ Distance between the Fur of the Hat and the Ball on the Hat
☐ Width of Head

Santa Vest

Item	Length of Fabric
Santa Vest Fabric	2.0 yards
Santa Vest Lining	2.0 yards

☐ Side Pockets - Left or Right or Both
☐ Wallet Pocket: Inside - Yes/No (Left or Right or Both)
☐ Chest measurements
☐ What type of fabric? (Silk, velvet, velveteen, cotton, etc.)
☐ Do you want to wear the vest with a stomach insert?
☐ Is there back adjustment strap?

Santa Pants

Item	Length of Fabric
Santa Pants 45 inches inseam - Velvet	2.5 yards
Santa Pants 60 inches inseam - Velvet	3.0 yards

Check-off List for Pants

- ☐ Side Pockets - Left or Right or Both
- ☐ Wallet Pocket: Yes/No (Left or Right or Both)
- ☐ Suspenders: Yes/No Buttons on the inside of pants
- ☐ Belt Loops for belt: Normal width 1 ¾
- ☐ Elastic at the waist of pants: Yes / No
- ☐ Elastic at the bottom of pants: Yes / No
- ☐ Waist measurement
- ☐ Inseam measurement
- ☐ Calf measurement
- ☐ Fur - decide removable or non-removable for the end of the pants

Notes:

Charles Howard Santa Suit
by
Elizabeth Babcock

Santa's Hat – Lined with silk, trimmed 6-inch band of French white rabbit pelts of fur with heavy white wool yarn ball on the end with 3 inches of braided wool connecting the woolen ball.

Wig – Needs to be shoulder length, made with Yak hair imported from China.

Beard - Made from Yak hair imported from China. Approximately 16 - 20 inches long.

Santa's Suit – Approximately 5 yards of 100% Red wool suit with 20 to 30 6-inch band of French white rabbit fur down the front, on the cuffs and large shawl collar. Elastic wrist-hugging cuffs.

Santa's Belt and Buckle - 4-inch black patent leather with eight - sided anodized 6-inch aluminum buckle which represents the 8 named reindeer in 1937.

Santa's Pants – Must Be knicker-style, while having a deep pocket on each side of the pants lined with red silk.

Santa's Boots - Made and lined with leather using 4-inch patent-leather.

This graphic is a compilation of information from newspaper interviews from the most well-known Santa Suit makers in the history of the Santa community.

Santa Claus/St. Nicholas Suit Measurements

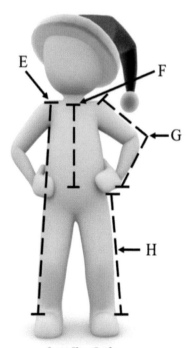

Santa Claus Outfit
(C) 2021 James Brown
All Rights Reserved

A -Head Measurements: Measure the circumference of the head at mid-brow level; just above the ears & eyebrows. If a wig is worn, include it in the measurement. (do not wear a hat). Please provide measurements in inches/centimeters:_____

B – Neckline Measurements: Measure the circumference of the neck at its base. Please provide measurements in inches/centimeters: _____

C – Chest Measurements: Measure the circumference of the chest at its fullest point. Do you wear padding? If so, take the measurement with the chest insert. Please provide measurements in inches/centimeters: _____

D – Waist Size (commonly known as Cookie Zone): Measure the circumference of the belly at its widest point; knicker-style pants will be held up by suspenders above the true waistline. Do you wear padding? If so, take the measurement with the padding insert. Please provide measurements in inches/centimeters: _____

E – Robe: Measure from the base of the neck to the heel. Do you wear padding? Yes No If so, take the measurement with the padding insert in inches/centimeters: _____

F – Coat/Shirt: Measure the middle of the back from the base of the neck to the top of leg. Do you wear padding? Yes No If so, take the measurement with the padding insert in inches/centimeters: _____

G – Sleeve Length: Continuing from "Top Shoulder," measure from the very top of the arm, where it meets the edge of the shoulder, to the base of the wrist, with elbow bent and forearm at a 90-degree angle in front of the body. If so, take measurements of including wig in inches/centimeters: _____

H – Outerseam: Measure the outer leg from the waistline to the top of the foot; knicker-style pants cling to the ankle with elastic, and are made to blouse over mid-calf boots. Please provide measurements in inches/centimeters: _____

Santa Claus Outfit
(C) 2021 James Brown
All Rights Reserved

131

Creating your Saint Nicholas Outfit

If you decide to either buy or have your outfit made by a seamstress, here are some basic facts about the actual outfit. There are many sources online to purchase your outfit. The information below pertains to making your own outfit.

There seem to be limited resources on making the outfit from scratch. You will need to pick one pattern to choose from:

1. **St. Nicholas Center** – St. Nicholas pattern (no modifications needed)
2. **McCall's Costumes #2339** (modifications needed)
3. **Simplicity #4795** (modifications needed)
4. **Simplicity # 4213** (modifications needed)

We would highly suggest that you go to the St. Nicholas Center to read up on their suggested modifications. In addition to picking out your pattern, it is highly suggested that you also purchase the following:

Simplicity #5840 (includes cape with a capelet option)
Butterick B5441 (includes two miter patterns)
Vestments for All Seasons (purchased from Amazon)

Description	Length of Fabric	Width of Fabric
Cape, capelet, stole and miter	9 ¾ yards	45 inches
Lining for cape	8 ¼ yards	54 inches
Interfacing for cape and capelet	2 ¾ yards	N/A
Interfacing for stole	1 ¾ yards	N/A
Interfacing for miter	1 ½ yards	20 inches
Gold braid/trim	3 ½ yards	N/A

Saint Nicholas Measurements

Please refer to the measurement graphic for the St. Nicholas measurements, as well as for the measurements for the Santa Suit.

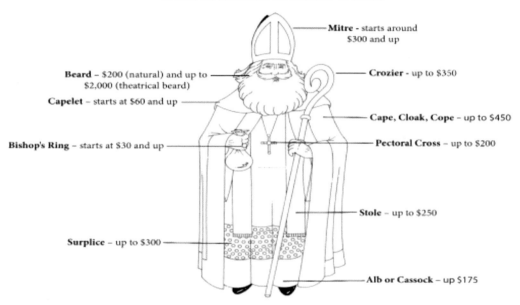

Cost of Saint Nicholas Outfit

Mitre - starts around $300 and up

Beard – $200 (natural) and up to $2,000 (theatrical beard)

Crozier - up to $350

Capelet – starts at $60 and up

Cape, Cloak, Cope – up to $450

Bishop's Ring – starts at $30 and up

Pectoral Cross – up to $200

Stole – up to $250

Surplice – up to $300

Alb or Cassock – up $175

St. Nicholas by Patrick Kelley, (C)1993, Daughters of St. Paul.
Used with Permission

Mrs. Claus Outfit

For those of you who have a partner willing and desiring to portray Mrs. Claus, here is some information to help you get started. A few basic facts about Mrs. Claus will also assist in developing the personality/character: Her first name is Jessica, and she has a knack for baking and matching toys with children on the Nice List.

Directions for resources and how to assemble a Mrs. Claus outfit are in Appendix B.

Basic Mrs. Claus Outfit Cost Breakdown

Mrs. Claus Hair –
$150 Natural Hair Highlights/
Up to $2,600 for a Human Wig

Glasses – Up to $300 a pair, if prescription

Makeup – Up to $200 per season

White Gloves –
Up to $20 per pair

Accessories – Up to $1,500

Custom Mrs. Claus Outfit – Up to $4,000

Mrs. Claus Shoes – Up to $300 a pair

© 2021 James Brown

Concluding Thoughts

Whether or not you choose to buy an off-the-rack suit, get a custom-made suit or make your own suit, the Santa suit is a major part of your Santa portrayal. First impressions are critical to the success of your business and having a Santa suit which fits well and is in great condition will help you tremendously with that first impression. Take time to consider each element of the suit and learn to properly care for your suit. Most importantly though, enjoy wearing it and the opportunities having the suit brings you!

Chapter 8

Santa's Make-up

"For Christmas is tradition time—
Traditions that recall
The precious memories down the years,
The sameness of them all."
— Helen Lowrie Marshall

Santa's Make-up

Santa's make-up needs to be simple and appear as natural as possible. No one wants a Santa that has caked on make-up. Most men do not use make-up on a regular basis and may have never used make-up at all. With the lack of experience and knowledge, it would be an excellent idea to go to a make-up professional to learn about the various products and techniques. Remember that practice builds confidence and reduce the time it takes to apply or remove make-up.

Personal Note: Portraying Santa was the first and only time I have ever had a make-over. I do recommend getting a make-over every couple of years. Your skin tone changes, so the colors you will use will also change. Santa needs to understand he needs to look his very best for the camera. Yes, in the end it did pay off.

So for your big day, ensure your skin is ready to begin the make-up process. Always prepare your skin by ensuring it is clean and dry. Try to make certain all the oil has been removed from your face prior to applying your make-up. Just remember that the product which works for one Santa is not always the right product for you. Experiment and find the best product for your skin. Always test the products first to find out if you have any reactions to the skin care and make-up products! This is particularly true for anyone who has skin sensitivities or known allergies to any of the ingredients listed in the products. Fortunately, there are many products available now which have been designed for people who tend to react to certain chemicals or ingredients used in the production of make-up and skin care merchandise. This is where makeovers can be very helpful in determining what works and is safe for you to use.

Personal Note: I keep my make-up down a very few items. Keep it simple.

1. Concealer
2. Foundation
3. Powder
    a. Setting Powders
    b. Face Powders
4. Eyes
    a. Charcoal pencil
    b. White eyeliner Pencil
5. Eyebrows
6. Checks and Nose
    a. Red blush

Here is a basic background of use of each item, plus others you may consider.

1. **Concealer** — Just remember concealer is what it is. The concealer's job is to cover up any blemish on your skin. According to the make-up industry a red/pink concealer is used to cover up dark or blue splotches on your skin. Blue-based concealers are used for redness or blemishes. Yellow-based concealers are used for blemishes such as freckles birthmarks, and even some tattoos.

2. **Foundation** — This is a liquid or powder makeup that is applied on the face to create an even uniformed color to cover up flaws in the skin or even to change the color of one's natural skin tone. Most foundations include a moisturizer, sunscreen, and additional applications for more complex cosmetics. Be careful and sparing with foundation, as too much or using the wrong color can create a caked on or clownish appearance. Make-up sponges are extremely helpful with liquid foundation, while a quality make-up brush will help with powder foundations.

3. **Red blush** — Dab the color onto the cheeks and the nose using your fingers or a damp sponge, blending well. Don't be afraid to go really rosy, as the face will not show much underneath the beard you will be putting on later and you want your Santa's face to look very pink. Be careful not to get this on your beard. Blush comes in powder form and in a more solid form, almost like a crayon or thick gel. You will need to experiment with the blush to determine how much color looks good and how much will give you a clownish appearance.

4. **White eyeliner pencil** — Use this to fill in or create lines on your face. Gently rub the white into your skin. This cosmetic can also be applied around the eyes to make them appear larger or more noticeable.

5. **Charcoal eyeliner pencil** — Use this to outline your eyes. Some people may also use mascara on eyelashes to achieve the same effect.

6. **Eyebrow pencil and brush** — This pencil is different than what you use on your eyes and should either match your eyebrow color or be slightly darker. An eyebrow brush is a tiny brush which will help "straighten" the eyebrow hairs to have a neater appearance for pictures.

7. **Lip balm** — Remember that the focus is on the rosy cheeks, not the lips!

Do not use much of this as it would gunk up the mustache and beard. Better to use this when you are in "civilian" mode. Also – Santas should avoid lipstick! This could stain the white hairs on mustache and beard, as well as gunk up the hairs like lip balm.

For stage makeup, the following companies have a reputation for providing a premium product:

Ben Nye
Ben Nye Makeup has been an industry standard makeup materials manufacturer for professionals in film and theatrical productions for decades. Ben Nye is talc based.

Mehron
Mehron was founded in 1927 by Mehron Melik. Mehron is well known for producing and innovating in areas such as character makeup kits, professional clown makeup, Halloween makeup as well as face and body painting makeup products among others. Mehron is glycerin based.

Concluding Thoughts

Which brands and shades of make-up and skin care should all be based to meet the needs of your skin type and coloring. Fortunately, nowadays there are foundations and products for sensitive skin types and also available to match almost every skin color and type, so no matter your heritage, you should be able to find what you need. Remember that generally, "less is more" when it comes to make-up!

Notes:

Chapter 9

Beards

Proper care and styling and presentation of Santa's hair goods leaves a great lasting memory of the Santa visit
— Thomas Sheerin

Beards

For this section: I could not have completed this section without the help of Thomas "Tom" Sheerin of East Weymouth, Massachusetts and an inductee of the International Santa Claus Hall of Fame. Tom is currently the lead expert of tradition beard sets for the Santa Community in the United States. His experience on this subject spans over 40 years. I am very thankful for Tom's help in writing this section of the book.

The question always comes with Santas which beard should I wear. For some Santas the question is just a question. Typically, you will make that decision on your own accord based upon your lifestyle.

Being a year-round Santa does have its perks but there are some down points. In many cases, real-beard Santas have more events to attend every year. They are normally underneath the public microscope every time they are in public. People tend to notice Santa-looking beards and may make vocal comments, especially children wondering why Santa isn't wearing his famous suit. This can lead to problems when trying to maintain a separation between being Santa and being a "civilian" or off-duty.

Sears, Roebuck, and Co. Catalog. Image courtesy of www.sears.com

Being a traditional beard Santa provides one the opportunity to enjoy his life without being a focal point of any occasion. Traditional beard Santas have the anonymity to move among others and enjoy living without being underneath a microscope.

Historically, traditional bearded Santas set the stage for today's Santa activities. C.W. Howard was a traditional bearded Santa and built his Santa school around the traditional beard. For instance, in the majority of the cities that host Thanksgiving Dayparades, the Santas use a traditional beard set. The traditional beards are aesthetically pleasing to the crowds and audiences. Each hair piece has its positives and drawbacks which could be mitigated with proper care and handling. The biggest items of concern for each Santa comes down to maintenance, expectations, desired aesthetics, and the purchasing budget.

Comparison of Theatrical Beards versus Natural Beards

	Theatrical Beard	Natural (Real) Beard
Positive	Look like a "Story Book Santa"	Many variations of a "Santa Look"
	Less Maintenance than Real Beard	Year-round marketing as Santa
	Nearly anyone can wear one	Warm in the winter/Hot in the summer
	Easy to hide from children/grandchildren	No shaving
	Anonymous	

	Theatrical Beard	Natural (Real) Beard
Negative	Short term expense - Purchase	Variations in Hair growth cycle
	Beard tugging customers/clients	Coloring (Bleaching)
	You still must shave	Food Staining
	Cleaning after each use	Natural Genetics on what you can grow

Historical Aspect of the Santa Beard

Have you ever wondered why Santa has a beard rather than is clean shaven? Many of us assume that Santa wears a beard based upon the Thomas Nast and Coca-Cola™ drawings of Santa. Did you know that the beard actually goes back to the historical meeting at the Ecumenical Councils?

Historians will always debate why Santa has a beard. However, theologians will direct you back to Saint Nicholas, the Greek-Turkish bishop in the early fourth century. As with any cultural debate, the church leadership was at the center, especially Roman Emperor Constantinople. Researchers believe that the Early Church Fathers such as Augustine of Hippo and Clement of Alexandria, both from North Africa, argued strongly for the beard.

During this time in history, the church was divided between Western Orthodox and Eastern Orthodox topics such as culture and heritage. In the Eastern Church, the bishops grew their beards to imitate Christ and His apostles and to keep the law of the Old Testament.

However, according to the *Catholic Encyclopedia*, the Western Church claims that Saint Peter instituted the new tonsure, which was shaving the top of the head and leaving a ring around the edges to signify the crown of thorns of Christ. In addition to the tonsure, the beard was shaved to show humility.

As a Bishop in the Eastern tradition, Saint Nicholas chose to follow the footsteps of Clement and Augustine which prevented him from shaving. This is why Saint Nicholas is traditionally depicted with a beard. According to historical documents, he lived a long life and following the traditional choices of his lifestyle, Saint Nicholas would have had a long white beard. This image was made part of the Sinterklaass tradition and became the basis of the modern-day Santa Claus.

Traditional (Theatrical) Beard Santa

The positives and drawbacks of each type of hair piece could be mitigated with proper care and handling. Each Santa needs to determine how much time, effort and money he is willing and able to put into becoming Santa when considering maintenance, expectations, desired aesthetics and budget. As Santa shops for his hair piece, he should have a basic knowledge of the different types. Please ensure that you make a wise decision on your hair piece prior to purchase to ensure that you are getting your money's worth. As a side note, it is recommended that you purchase additional mustaches and eyebrows with your set to match.

Parts of a Traditional Beard Set

Santa Claus wig sets commonly consists of head piece, beard, mustache, and eyebrows.

Beards typically come in separate pieces or as one piece sets. The higher quality sets will normally be separate pieces where the cheaper sets are normally one piece.

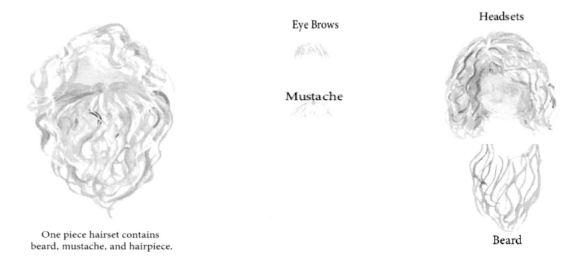

One piece hairset contains beard, mustache, and hairpiece.

Eye Brows

Mustache

Headsets

Beard

Comparsion of Traditional Beard Set

Positives	Human Hair	Yak Hair	Synthetic Sets
Care	X	X	X
Adaptability	X	X	
Texture	X	X	
Longevity	X	X	
Natural Look	X	X	
Resilent	X	X	
Styling & Retention	X	X	X
Cost			X

Negatives	Human Hair	Yak Hair	Synthetic Sets
High Maintenance	X	X	
Cost to purchase	X	X	
Reacts to Weather	X	X	
Color Fading	X	X	
Weight	X	X	
Styling	X	X	
Shine			X
Less Versatility			X
Can't Change Color			X
Texture			X
Longevity			X

Human Hair Sets

Many Santas use the human hair wig and/or animal hair sets. Both sets offer the same styling versatility of real hair. This feature is both the pros and the cons of a human hair wig. Because human hair wigs are made of real hair, they require much more maintenance, styling and upkeep. Without the natural oils from your scalp to condition the wig, they can get dry and brittle without proper maintenance. Just like your own hair, they will lose their style in the rain or humidity and must be restyled. They are also much more expensive than synthetic wigs. In contrast, one of the great benefits to a synthetic wig is that your hair always looks good with almost no effort. Another benefit to all human hair sets are handmade according to your head measurements.

Pros:

Adaptability —Human hair wigs can be colored, permed and styled just like your own hair. If needed, take your wig to a stylist who is experienced in dealing with human hair wigs so you will be less likely to develop permanent snags.

Longevity — With proper care, human hair wigs can last two to three times longer than synthetic wigs.

Natural Look/Texture — Human hair wigs feel great and can look incredibly natural, due to its texture being actual human hair.

Easier to style — You can use rollers, hair dryer (low heat), and curling iron if needed.

Cons:

High Maintenance — Just like real hair, human hair wigs need to be washed, deep-conditioned and re-styled frequently. Styling is much more labor intensive, requiring styling skills and increased time/effort.

Lace is damaged quickly due to the lack of cleaning — The lace can become damaged due to the lack of properly cleaning and removing adhesive.

Cost — Since the hair is harvested from other humans, they are typically more expensive.

Reacts to Weather — Just like your own hair, this type of wig will react to the weather and can become frizzy, limp or dry depending on the weather.

Fragile — The hair will incur damage if subjected to harsh brushing, back-combing or overuse of heated styling tools.

Weight — Human hair wigs can feel heavier than synthetic wigs of a similar length and style.

Color Fading — The color of a human hair wig will oxidize or fade with exposure to light.

YAK Hair Sets

Yak Hair – Yak hair is NOT human hair. It is harvested from the body of the Yak animal – an ox-like mammal native to the Himalayas and Tibet with dark, long and silky hair, a horse-like tail and a full, bushy mane. The hair of the yak is structurally like human hair. Testing revealed that it responded the same way to the styling methods used to style human hair as human hair responded. Yak hair has become widely used in the industry. Please understand that some people are allergic to the yak fibers, similarly to people allergic to cat or dog hair. The more expensive yak hair sets are handmade.

Crepe Hair – Also called wool crepe, this is commonly used for beards, eyebrows, or mustaches. Each hair is individually glued to the face. This product is normally sold in wrapped in tight braid hair that unravels wavy. Crepe hair needs to be washed and combed straighten prior to use. Lay it out flat to dry, otherwise it will be curly.

Pros:

Yak hair is **very natural** and **realistic.**

Longevity — Life expectancy of the hair set is based upon how well the knots are constructed. Single knot lace will have a shorter life. With proper care, human hair wigs can last two to three times longer than synthetic wigs. Also, hot water will loosen the knots.

Resilient — Yak hair is more resilient to the weather such as humidity and dampness because it is made from animal hair vice human hair.

Easy to refresh and restore to the design you prefer.

Cons:

Permanently snags —Yak hair is more likely to develop snags while washing and shampooing.

More expensive than other synthetic hair, but less than a human hair set.

Lace is damaged quickly due to the lack of cleaning — The lace can become damaged due to the lack of cleaning and removing adhesive.

Scratchy texture by nature.

Fading — Heat will cause the hair to yellow. It is best to store the set in cool and dark conditions.

Allergies — Some people will react to yak hair similarly to cat or dog hair.

Synthetic Sets

Many people who have not seen a high-quality synthetic wig think that they need a human hair wig to get a natural look. This is simply not the case. Synthetic wigs have the benefit of retaining their shape, so they require little styling. Simply spritz the wig with a spray bottle of water, and the hair will return to its original style.

Synthetic sets are considered inferior quality, greyish in color, and difficult to style. These sets are normally the sets you purchase at the local Halloween stores and worn with costumes. Another negative to synthetic hair is that it cannot be exposed to heat sources as the heat will permanently damage the fibers. Therefore, you cannot use a curling iron, flat iron, hair dryer or other heated styling tools on the wig.

Polypropylene is one the cheapest sets of beards that come with Santa outfits such as Rubies and department stores. This type is not flame retardant so it should never be subjected to heat at any time. Because of its limitations and dangers, the hair industry has decided to phase this material out of the hair extensions market. These sets are normally found at costume shops or are included in Santa sets found in department stores and typically sell for less than $100.00.

Pros:

> **Easy Care** — Synthetic wigs are easy to take care of. Because synthetic wigs have something called "style retention," they never have to be styled. You simply wash, dry and then shake them out, and the wig will return to its initial factory-formed style.

> **Style Memory** — Synthetic wigs hold their style regardless of the weather.

> **Cost** — Synthetic wigs are significantly less expensive than human hair or yak hair sets.

Low Maintenance – They require very little maintenance.

Longevity – Synthetic wigs and toppers last longer as human/yak hair wigs.

Cons:

Does not photograph well – These sets normally do not photograph well since the whiskers are synthetic and hollow, when a light is flashed on them, the wig can put a fiber optic design on Santa's face.

Shine – Some economy or budget synthetic wigs (typically those under $100) may have an unnatural shin

Less Versatility – Synthetic wigs cannot be straightened or curled with heated styling tools unless it is a specifically designed "heat-friendly" synthetic wig.

Basic Supplies and Tools for Wig Care

We have come up with a list of items that you may need to the care of your wig sets – whether you are just storing them or you will be cleaning and styling your wig yourself. Just remember that you need to have a clean, cool, dry, and dark place to store your wig on a head block. Here are the following items:

Display Mount – It is important to use with the canvas head. This helps keeps the canvas block head from falling over. You can make the display mount of anything for your mannequin head.

Wide Tooth Comb – This is used for smoothing, detangling and styling. It works well if you have two on hand, with one at your dressing studio and one for your travel bag. These can be purchased at most drugstores or beauty supply shops, usually from $1 to $6.

Blocking Tape (Twill Tape) and Pins – In order to protect, store, comb, or style the wig or beard, you will need to use blocking tape and pins to hold your wig in place. You will need to "block" the lace front on a canvas head using twill tape. This stabilizes that delicate lace, keeps it from pulling or warping and ensures that the tension you put on the wig to comb it will not tear your lace or put holes in it. Use the finest pins you can find, typically sold as "silk pins". When dealing with a wet head of hair, it is recommended to use ½ inch elastic blocking tape.

Canvas Block Head (Mannequin Head)/Styrofoam Male Head/Beard Block

Styrofoam head blocks are inexpensive and can work satisfactorily. However, canvas block heads in your head size will keep the firm fit you need for your head piece. Depending upon your financial situation, you can store facial hair on the block with your wig or purchase a second canvas block for your beard. There are plenty of online retailers such as Amazon and brick and mortar stores who sell this product.

(Optional) **Mannequin Head Carrying Case** – A carrying case will allow you to carry your mannequin head without anyone suspecting that you are Santa. There are several sets of instructions online for you to use or you can purchase a carrying case. Ensure that the case fits the length of your beard.

Rollers – Rollers are optional because if you send your hair piece out for styling you can bypass this step. However, it is good to have them available in a pinch. Rollers can be either rigid or foam, depending on your preference.

Wool Daubers – The wool applicator is used for removing liquid adhesive and tape from hair sets and face. It will not leave fibers or dyes that can contaminate the primer and compromise its effectiveness. The thin metal handle provides the right blend of durability and flexibility for even application. A hook at the end helps prevent drops that can contaminate the dauber.

(Optional) **Afro comb** (commonly referred as Afro pic - An afro comb/pick is a large comb designed with big, wide teeth to get into tightly curled hair and lift it up without destroying the curl.

(Optional) **Metal Wave Clamps** – Metal Wave Clamps are used in conjunction with rollers for styling your hair piece. These clamps have a great grip and are vented for faster drying time. Ensure they are plastic coated.

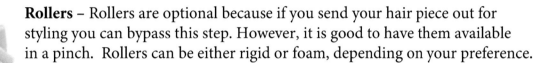

(Optional) **T-pins** – T-pins are used to anchor down your rollers.
Note: Do not use T-Pins in the front lace section of your hair piece.

(Optional) **Duckbill Clips** – Duckbill Clips are long, slim clips that are great for holding sections of hair during styling or cutting. These clips are sleek enough to blend with any outfit while keeping the hair locked in place all day long. Only use alumin clips – any other clips will rust and leave the metal oxidation on your hair piece.

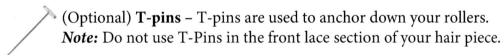

Storage of Hair Pieces

If your pieces are made from synthetic, yak hair or human hair, the pieces are all affected by the same issues your personal hair will suffer from such as moisture, humidity, sunlight, etc. As discussed earlier, avoid storing your hair pieces in humid conditions or direct sunlight.

Use of Hair Nets

Between events, the easiest way to preserve the style of your wig, especially if it is long and/or curly, is to use large bouffant hair nets to support your wig or beard. Hair nets contain the entire hair piece and help to retain shape and curls. As soon as you have completed your event, put the headpieces on your canvas head block. Once your headpiece is secured, take the wide toothed plastic comb and comb the headpieces to eliminate tangles. Simply stretch the net to cradle the hair and use a straight pin to secure the net to your block. (***Note:*** Use a separate hairnet for your headpiece and beard.)

Storage of a Hair Set

During the off season, your hair pieces need to be stored in a cool, dry, and dark acid free area. Yak and Human hair sets can turn yellow if left in the sunlight. Another storage method to consider is to cover them with a breathable cloth to allow air circulation. Below is a mockup a basic hair stand.

Do It Yourself Head Stand

This example was constructed for less than $20.00.

Required Items:

— Styrofoam male mannequin head. This can be found at any craft store or online for under $10.
— Wood base – 2x4 approximately 6-inches long.
— PVC pipe approximately 4 inches long with a diameter of 1 inch.(Measure before starting – PVC pipe for the head stand must be long enough that the beard is suspended not touching the base of the wood).
— Wood Glue

Step 1 — Purchase or acquire all the supplies needed.

Step 2 — Drill a hole in the scrap wood the same diameter of the PVC piping.

Step 3 — Place PVC piping in the wood base. Place wood glue around the PVC pipe and base. Let it dry complete.

Step 4 — Put PVC pipe into the base of the mannequin head.

Step 5 — To keep dust off hair piece, use an old pillowcase which allows the air to follow around your hair piece.

Trying on Your Beard or Other Facial Hair

Like your wig, as soon as your beard or facial hair arrives in the mail, you need to remove the item from the box and try it on. The best place to put it on is in front of the mirror. Also, I would suggest that Mrs. Claus, or your Elf assistant, help place the wig and beard on your head and face for the first fitting.

There are two different types of straps for hair pieces. One uses elastic and the other uses non-elastic adhesive. You need to determine which type is easier to use and holds more efficiently for you.

Elastic Strip Beard — Put your beard at the top of your head and gently pull down over your face. Then place your chin in the chin cup. Properly adjust your straps until the beard is snug on your face. Gently adjust the remainder of your beard for the proper look.

Non-Elastic Strap Beard — This will be tricky the first time that you use this type of beard. There are two options to check to see if the beard will properly fit.

1. Hold the beard in place with your hand so you can look at it in the mirror.

2. You can place double-sided toupee tape on either the top of the beard or any other place you feel comfortable while you look at it in the mirror.

Every wig set will have excess lace on the wig and beard set. Do not trim the edge off until you have tried the beard on and are pleased with the overall look. The extra is provided to add additional hair to the lace, creating a fuller or longer beard.

Mustache —

1. Hold the mustache in place with your fingers so you can look at it.

2. You can place double sided toupee tape on the back of your mustache while you look at it.

Proper Fitting — Beards should have a very symmetrical appearance. Position your beard and hair piece properly. Adjust your beard and wig appropriately by scooting it down until it fits properly.

A Few Things to Keep in Mind About Wearing your Wig or Beard

Practice, practice, practice putting your wig and beard! Please do not wait until the day of your event to put on your outfit. You will make mistakes which will make you late to your event or even worse, you could ruin your outfit by having to rush.

You have heard the cliche, "there's no one-size-fits all." One piece of advice from other Santa's: The biggest factor to consider regarding wigs or beards is that everyone's body is different. Some people have oily skin, while some have dry skin. Please make trial runs with your pieces to see what works best for you, in your particular situations. This will ensure that you know what supplies you need to keep on hand and how long you need to get ready for Santa visits.

Just remember, the glue or tape that your friend recommends for them may not work at all for you. Also, remember that a glue which works well for you indoors, might not work well outdoors or in the summer. Please test your application products in the similar environment that your performance could take place. Practice, practice, practice.

Types of Liquid Adhesive

Regarding wig applicators, you can purchase these items from any store that sells wigs, or you may purchase these items from Amazon. If your locality has a wig store, stop in and discuss your needs with them and allow them to direct you to specific products and application tips which might be useful for you.

Remember when using glue – *"Less glue is better."*

There are multiple types of hair adhesives:

Spirit Gum Glue – Spirit gum is used primarily for affixing costume prosthetics such as wigs or false facial hair. It has been around since the 1870s and has long been a standard tool in theatrical performances where prosthetic makeup or affixed costuming is used. *Tip:* When you purchase a new bottle of glue, remove the cap of the bottle for a couple of hours to allow the alcohol in the glue to dissolve prior to use.

Toupee Glue – Toupee Glue is designed to be a waterproof adhesive holds thru sweat, water, and an oily scalp. The glue is advertised to be dependable multipurpose bonding waterproof hairpiece adhesive.

Liquid hair Glues – These acrylic or silicone-based glues which help to attach wigs or weaves to the hairline. It is semi-permanent glue and lasts for 6 weeks. **Warning:** Use of this type of hair glue is NOT recommended as you will be stuck wearing your hair pieces until the glue eventually wears off, in about 6 weeks!

Keratin Glue – This type comes in semi-hard chips and is used to bond the hair extension weft, weave onto scalp. It is expensive and removal is difficult.

Ultra-hold Glue – Ultra hold glue is perhaps the most popular lace front wigs glues available. It can give you a strong hold for three to four weeks. It is recommended for people that have not had any luck with other types of glues.

Invisibond Glue– Invisibond is a water-based glue that will give you about 2 to 3 weeks hold. It comes as a white liquid but dries on clear to give you a waterproof strong bond. Invisibond is especially recommended for people new to lace-front wigs glue and do not know which one to initially try.

Vapon No Tape Glue – It comes as a clear liquid. Vapon No Tape Glue also dries clear giving you a strong waterproof bond. It should be used with extreme care as it hardly allows any room for mistakes. This is a great glue for people who profusely sweat or experience hot flashes producing sweat.

How to Apply Liquid Adhesive

In today's world, they are many ways to adhere your traditional beard to your face. You will need to test each adhesive out until you find the right combination which works well for your skin.

NOTE: DO NOT DRINK ALCOHOL WITHIN THE PAST 12 HOURS – this will impact the durability of the adhesive and allow the adhesive not to work.

Required Items:

Wool Daubers/small craft paint brushes
Clean Dry wash rag
Liquid Adhesive of your choice

Step 1 — Clean your face with the rubbing alcohol. Ensure you do not get into your eyeballs.

Step 2 — Wait until your skin is dry before placing the adhesive on your face.

Step 3 — Apply the adhesive evenly to the skin with wool Daubers/small craft paint brushes. ***Note:*** Remember that a little bit goes a long way, so it is better to use a small amount of adhesive. Allow it to dry which means it will be tacky on your skin.

Step 4 — Apply the adhesive evenly to the eyebrows or mustache. Once the adhesive is tacky on the hair piece it is ready be placed on your face.

Step 5 — Apply your beard, then head piece and finally mustache. Place mustache on upper lip, not directly below the nose, for a more natural appearance. Hold until secure on your face.

Step 6 — If there is any break in securing the piece, then use a drop or two in the gap areas to ensure it adheres evenly to the skin.

Step 7 — Use a rag with adhesive remover to remove any unwanted glue.

How to Remove Your Mustache and Eye Brows

Required Items:

91% Rubbing Alcohol/Manufacture Adhesive Remover
Wool daubers

Step 1 — Remove your Suit Jacket, Stocking Hat and any other accessories.

Step 2 — Place small amount adhesive remover on the wool dauber. Take the dauber and dab around the hair piece and gently tap the hair until it becomes easy to remove.

Step 3 — Gently remove your mustache. Allow time for the 91% Rubbing Alcohol/ Manufacture Adhesive Remover to work. Otherwise, you will stretch out the lace, which usually results in the lace not retaining the shape and the knots possibly coming apart.

Step 4 — Repeat steps 2-4 until the hair piece has been removed.

Step 5 — Once the hairpieces are removed from your skin, wash your face with soap and use moisturizer if needed.

Step 6 — Once the hairpiece is removed from your face continue to remove the adhesive from the backside of the lace with the wool daubers and adhesive remover until it is completely removed. Gently rub the adhesive off with your fingers without stretching the lace. Allow the hair piece to dry.

How to Apply Tape

Required Items:

91% Rubbing Alcohol or Witch Hazel
Toupee Tape
Traditional Beard with Mustache and Eyebrows

Step 1 — Wipe your face down with the Rubbing Alcohol or Witch Hazel. You can use a clean washcloth or wool daubers. Note: Do not get this in your eyes.

Step 2 — Ensure that the pieces of the tape will match your face. Recommend that you pre-cut your pieces of adhesive tape prior to attaching the product to your face.

Step 3 — Attach the tape to your mustache and beard prior to attaching to your face. Ensure the tape is secured to your hair by using the back side of a small spoon or mini-icing spatula to rub the tape on the lace side of the hair piece.

Step 4 — Put your beard on first. Ensure the tape is not showing through your beard.

Step 5 — Place head piece in place. Attach the head piece to the tape.

Step 6 — Place your mustache on your upper lip, not right under your nose. Then securely attach mustache in place.

Step 7 — Put on your eyebrows. Ensure the tape is not outside the size or shape of the eyebrows. Then securely attach eyebrows in place.

Maintenance on a Traditional (Theatrical) Beard

Required Items:

Theatrical Beard
Baby Shampoo and Conditioner or Lottabody
Foam Rollers
Wide Tooth Comb
Hair Pick
Unscented Hair Spray
Optional — Mannequin Head (prefer cork or Styrofoam)
Optional — Pins

Directions:

Step 1 — Once you have purchased a Theatrical that has extra lace, it is recommended that once you have tried it on, you trim down the lace to on the eyebrows and mustaches down to 1/16 of an inch. The beard and wig should be trimmed down to ½ inch of the lace.

Step 2 — It is recommended that the Theatrical Beard should be washed in Baby Shampoo and conditioner in cold water. Rinse in cold water. *(Personal preference:* Pin the wig to the Mannequin Head before washing. This helps with keeping the shape of the headpiece and beard). Place the head in a pan of water. Do not make rapid movements in the water. This could cause the wig to become tangled. (*Note:* Most synthetic sets curl will come back after drying, yak sets however lose all the curl once wet or combed wet).

Step 3 — Dry the set by shaking the water off and using the pat method with a towel.

Step 4 —Use foam rollers while the hair is still damp after washing it. Allow the wig to dry completely with the rollers in. After the wig is dry carefully remove all the rollers.

Step 5 — Once your hair set is completely dry, work on the detangling the curls. Carefully "comb out" your wig. You can use Baby Detangler spray to help with the tangles. Use a wide tooth comb or your fingers starting at base of the wig and work your way down.

Step 6 — Spray the hair piece and beard with unscented hairspray.

Word of Caution — Synthetic beards can be damaged by the heat from hot hairdryers. Synthetic hair will melt under high heat. So only use low or cool settings and not up close to the hair.

Treat human/yak hair beards like your own hair. Never store hair pieces in plastic bags. Store them out of direct sunlight and in a cool environment. Only store the sets once they are cleaned. Never store them in a dirty condition, including any glue residue from the season or hair spray.

Quick Cleaning on Hairpiece

Essential Care

1. Make-up will stain your hair piece. Clean this as soon as possible with rubbing alcohol to minimize staining or buildup.

2. Stains on the hairpieces.
   A. Wipe with a damp washcloth.
   B. If stain remains, then apply a tiny bit of shampoo. Let is set for a few minutes, then rinse.

3. Washing your hair piece and beard. The less you wash your hairpieces the longer these pieces will last. If financially feasible, consider purchasing multiple sets to reduce the amount of washing.

Note: Never soak or submerge your hair piece or beard in a bucket of solution. This will cause the hair to swell and become saturated. If this happens, the long-term effect will cause the hair knots to loosen.

4. Deodorizing Wig
   A. Lay the headpiece on its back with the inside facing up.
   B. Lightly mist the wig with a spray bottle that contains with water and small amount of rubbing alcohol.
   C. Let wig dry.
   D. Store as usual.

5. Heat Styling Tools
   A. Refrain from using excessive heat styling tools on either human, yak or synthetic hair.
   B. Using heat styling tools will cause the hair ends to slowly dry them out and damage them, ultimately leading to breakage.

6. Cleaning Glue (discussed in detail later in this chapter)

Santa Mustache Maintenance

Remember the following is a suggested way to clean your mustache and keep it looking fresh. Everyone's mustache is different in style/look, type and preferred adhesive. Most adhesives can be removed with just a little spritz of rubbing alcohol and blotting with a paper towel. However, for stubborn glue or stains use a soft toothbrush with small gentle circular motions on the back of the lace. You can remove extra hairspray and makeup using this method.

Restyling the Mustache

Suggested directions:

Step 1 — Pin your mustache to the canvas head using tape along the lace with small pins. Then spritz the hair, not the lace with water.

Step 2 — Comb the hair with a fine-toothed comb. Be extremely careful not to damage the knots that hold the hair.

Step 3 — Fold your mustache in half when working on it to ensure the same work is reflected on each side. Once you have finished combing out the mustache, take a hard roller and wrap the end of the mustache around the roller. Use the rollers to design your mustache as you desire. Once you have the rollers at the desire place, use pins to keep the rollers in place as the mustache dries. Remember to do one side at a time so you can fine tune the detail. ***Note:*** if your mustache is too short for rollers, please use pins to make the necessary adjustments.

Step 4 — Once the mustache has dried, remove the rollers and gently comb out the mustache with a fine-tooth comb and/or teasing brush. As you are combing out one side of your mustache, use this time to style it to the preferred look; then use pins to hold it in place. Repeat for the other side. ***Note:*** Speeding up the drying process with hair dryers can damage the hair.

Step 5 — You may use a small amount of fragrance-free hair spray or styling wax to help hold the hair it in place.

Step 6 —Attach mustache to Styrofoam as seen in photo provided.

Trimming the Wig Lace

Once you have decided you like how your wig fits, then you can trim the lace by to at least 3/8" wherever possible. Remember there could be sections on your hair that will need to be shorter, use your discretion. Use sharp scissors and cut in tiny increment. Remember to take your time making the cuts: Once cut, you cannot put it back on!

Important Tip: Please understand that cutting the lace close to the knots will increase the possibility of hair loss along the knotted edge.

If you have any questions or concerns about trimming your lace, please do not hesitate to reach out to other Santa's for their advice.

Hiding the Lace Edge of the Beard and Head Piece

Do's:

> — Try to blend the lace against the skin.
> — Put your lace on properly.
> — Glue or tape down the edges as needed

Don'ts:

> — Please do not roll the lace edge underneath. This will cause a bumpy and fake appearance. In the end, your lace will become damaged.
>
> — Do not cover the lace up with make-up. The make-up will make the lace more noticeable.

Adding Additional Hair Over Lace Edge
(Writeup and photo credit: Thomas Sheerin)

Required Items:

> Loose Yak Hair
> Small Paint Brush
> Spirit Glue
> Scissors

Step 1 — Start with about 3-inch piece of loose Yak hair, scissors, and brush with spirit gum. Use your scissors and cut the yak hair on a slight angle.

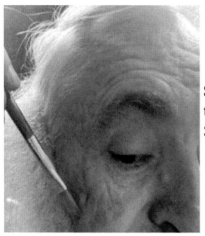

Step 2 — Apply spirit gum to your paint brush, then apply the spirit gum just above the lace line of the beard. Repeat Steps 1 and 2 for each side.

Step 3 — Before applying the hair, ensure the glue is tacky before pressing the loose hair into glue. Use the handle of the paint brush to press the hair into place. Allow the glue to dry before gently pulling away any hair that did not stick to the face.

Step 4 — Continue adding spirit gum and loose hair along and above the lace line. This is done on both sides to achieve your desired look.

Step 5 — The loose hair has now hidden the lace line or the hard edge when wearing a non-lace beard. If there are spots that need more, simply add a bit of sprit gum and press in some additional hair.

Concluding Thoughts

Thomas Sheeran has graciously contributed his experience and expertise to help so many Santas, in person and through this chapter. Wearing and caring for hair pieces can be tricky, especially for beginners. It is strongly recommended that you practice this when you are not rushed for time, so if you do make mistakes, you have time to fix them or start over. As you grow accustomed to the process of applying and removing hair pieces, it will get easier, and you will need less time. Do not neglect the proper care and storage of your hair pieces. Being able to use the same pieces for several seasons saves you the cost of frequent replacements. Above all, enjoy the transformation from your everyday self into the Santa whom everyone recognizes!

Notes:

Chapter 10

Natural Beards

Christmas to me is as many people as possible happy.
— Tupac Shakur

Natural Beards aka "Real Bearded Santas" Beard Care

For Santas who choose to grow their own beard and mustache instead of using hair pieces, you will need to pay special attention to cleaning, styling and trimming during the holiday season. Those Santas who have worn beards and mustaches prior to becoming Santa will be familiar with the information provided in this section regarding beard/mustache care. Remember that it takes time to grow out sufficient hair to have a neat appearance, so do not wait until fall to begin this process.

Required items for beard/mustache care:
>   Beard balm and/or beard oil
>   Beard comb and brush
>   Beard shampoo
>   Beard pomade
>   Beard trimming/styling kit

1. Beard Balm — Beard balm is designed to site on your beard and skin to provide more nourishing and long-lasting moisture to your beard. Beard balm acts as styling agent. The balm can help style those whiskers to provide a more finished touch. Both balm and beard oil do moisturize the skin under your beard; however, the balm stays longer on the skin to provide protection from the elements.

2. Beard Comb — A beard comb is one of the most important facets of beard care. Take your time to pick the correct comb for your beard. Ensure your comb has the right teeth spacing with anti-static and durable materials. Plastic combs tend to break, while most metal combs are uneven and can damage your facial hair and have been known to leave a static charge. Thus the choice of comb is a personal choice based on what works best for you.

3. Wide-toothed Comb — A wide tooth comb is generally better for men with massive beards (1 to 3-year length). The finer teethed combs can cause snags for your longer beards but can make your beard look much straighter.

4. Beard Brush — Beard brushes are designed for shorter beards to help distribute beard oils, leaning and massaging your beard; detangling, and styling. You should also brush your mustache with a beard brush.

5. Beard Oil — Beard oil hydrates the skin and will help soften and tame the beard. In some instances, the oil will help as a styling agent. The best time to apply the oil is first thing after showing or cleansing. The oil is absorbed more quickly into the skin versus the beard balm. As a result of the rapid absorption, the oil provides a finished appearance on the beard. Please ensure that you use a beard brush or comb to distribute the oil evenly across the beard.

6. Beard Shampoo — Beard shampoos are designed not to use the harmful chemicals that strip out your natural sebum oils. It is recommended that you wash your beard on each day when you will be performing as Santa. A recent study conducted by Switzerland's Hirslanden Clinic concluded that "men's beards contained more harmful bacteria in human whiskers than in dog fur."[45]

7. Beard Soap — Beard soap looks like a bar of soap; however, the soap is formulated for the facial hair with more moisturizing ingredients that hydrate the skin and beard while gently removing dirt and excess oil. Beard soap is generally less harsh on your beard than shampoo.

8. Beard Hair Pomade — The reason why men use pomade is that pomade gave the hair a dark, slicker, shinier appearance, while wax gave a looser, more texturized and matte finish. On the downside, however, you will need several washes to get this product of your hair.

9. Beard Trimming Scissors/Electric Trimmer — If you have recently grown a beard, you will want to practice using trimming scissors and/or an electric trimmer. This way, if you wind up making mistakes, you have time to grow the beard/mustache back out again. During the Christmas season, you may need to trim your beard and mustache into a neater style than you may choose to have in the off-season. Remember to check with a professional stylist prior to the use of any tools for the first time.

Additional tools you will need for styling, depending on the length of your beard and mustache include a hairdryer, mini-curling iron, hot rollers and unscented hairspray. Specific directions for beard and mustache care and styling are provided in Appendix C.

Bleaching vs Coloring

The majority of Santas in the business currently bleach their beards. Yes, having a real beard does command more money and more business opportunities at Christmas time. However, you must take the time to weigh the cost benefit factors of having a real beard. This is a tough personal and professional decision for Santas to make in the beginning of their careers, so think this through before making your decision.

Bleaching
Just remember that bleaching (or lifting) strips your hair of its natural color, so any darker color turns lighter. Bleaching removes the melanin from your hair, which makes the hair dry out and become brittle. Bleach damage is just as cumulative as it is permanent, and the ends of your hair will be less equipped to survive it every time.

Tip: To avoid bleaching mishaps, it's best to consult a professional colorist. If you are bleaching at home, please use swimmers ear plugs to keep the chemicals out of your ears and be sure not to get this in your eyes. The smell of bleach can be rather strong so make certain you are in a well-ventilated area while bleaching your hair.

Dyeing

Dyeing your hair is normally reserved for those who want to significantly change their hair color. Basically, with hair dye, your hair cuticle is opened, and the color pigments penetrate the hair follicles in order to create the color you prefer. Coloring is considered permanent until your hair roots grow out. This also means you must touch up the roots every few weeks to hide your natural color.

Note: Dyed hair cannot be dyed lighter.

Normally a semi-permanent color is less damaging than permanent color or bleaching (lifting), unless you are required to do a full bleaching process to change your color. Semi-permanent dyes will last for a good while, but eventually will fade out.

Tip: Reds always fade more quickly and can change to an orangey tone. Professional help is strongly recommended particularly for red hair dyes.

Permanent color is designed to go deeper in the hair strand. The permanent color contains peroxide when means the hair does get bleached. However, during this process, the color is being deposited which makes the hair follicle the new color. Unless a full bleaching process is required to change the hair color, permanent dyes are less damaging than lifting/bleaching.

More details and information on coloring/bleaching at home are provided in Appendix D. Always remember to consult your hair stylist/barber about this process to see what would work best for you, and whether it is best to have the professional do the coloring/bleaching or if you could attempt it at home on your own.

Concluding Thoughts

The decision to bleach and/or color your natural hair is a highly personal choice, and one with which you will have to live for a long time. Consult a professional before making any decisions and learn about post-bleaching and post-coloring hair care because any chemical processes used on your natural hair will change and possibly damage your hair.

Chapter 11
The Nitty Gritty

Let your "Ho! Ho! Ho!" not "Go! Go! Go!" this year.
— Anthony T. Hincks

The Nitty Gritty (All Santas Should Know)

Here is a list of Frequently Asked Questions (FAQs) that Santas should know.

How many children and homes are there in the world?

In 2019, according to the United Nations, there are approximately 1.9 billion children (ages 0 — 14) in the world. We do know that Santa does not visit every child in the world due to religious and theology issues. The elves have estimated that Santa does visits on average approximately 1.3 billion children each year.

How much coal does Santa hand out? How much is spent on coal?

To answer these questions, you need to know there are approximately 1.3 billion children who celebrate Christmas and anticipate a visit from Santa. Based upon a simple test on honesty and integrity, about 21% of the children who participated in the test displayed a rather disappointing lack of these esteemed character qualities. If you do the math, the results show approximately 273 million children will be on the Naughty List and can expect to receive a lump of coal in their stocking.

If each lump of coal weighs about 1 pound and **273,000,000** children will each get a lump, then Santa will deliver close to **136,500 tons of coal** every year! At the retail price of $6 per 1 pound lump, Santa must plan for $1,638,000,000 (**$1.638 billion**) in his budget for coal on an annual basis!

Santa's Sleigh

We need to mention here that the blueprints for Santa's Sleigh is considered *"TOP SECRET"* by the Santa Workshop Special Delivery Department. It is believed that the truss of the sleigh is made from a special titanium alloy that is very lightweight and is ten to twenty times stronger than anything we have today. We do know that the seat is made of velour, which is soft and very comfortable.

Santa's sleigh is equipped with state-of-the-art electronics which includes laser sensors, Federal Aviation Administration (FAA) flight equipment and the global positional System (GPS). It is believed that the GPS system on the sleigh informs him if the child is naughty or nice before he lands on the roof. Santa has a state-of-the-art radio which keeps him in constant touch with Mrs. Claus and the elves at the North Pole. The elves send him minute-to-minute updates on local weather reports and toy inventory.

How long does it take to transit the earth as Santa?

Santa Claus has a lot of work to do on Christmas Eve. On Dec. 24th, the sun sets in the Gilbert Islands (just west of the International Date Line) at 6:29 p.m. But it is useful when considering that the sun rises on Howland Island to the east of the Gilbert Islands which are on the other side of the date line. On Dec. 25th, the sun rises there at 5:44 a.m. — giving Santa 35 hours and 15 minutes of darkness to complete his task. This gives Santa enough time to work due to the different time zones and rotation of the Earth, of course, assuming that his journey is from east to west.

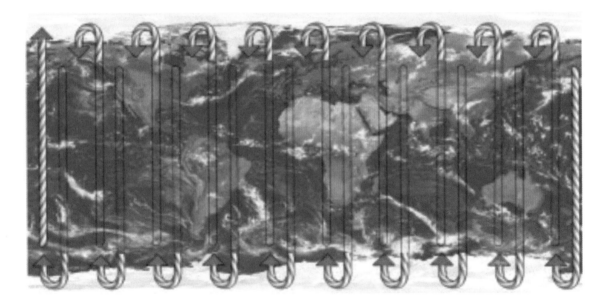

After leaving the North Pole, Santa travels the International Date until he stops at Christmas Island, the off the to the Island of Fuji. Santa continues onto New Zealand and Australia. Santa's reindeer take a quick break in Australia while Santa uses six white boomer kangroos. After a quick stop at the beach in Australia, he completes his trip to the islands before heading to Japan, Asia, then across to the Middle East, off to Europe and going to Africa before continuing to the Iceland. He stops in South America before heading to Canada and the United States and finally heads to Alaska before finishing up at the International Date where he started before going home.

How much time does Santa have to visit each home?

Based on today's nuclear family, it is estimated that 2.7 children live in each home which gives us roughly 565,217,391 homes to visit each night. If you convert 35 hours and 15 minutes to seconds that gives us 126,900 seconds. Santa has less than 1/1000 of a second to park his sleigh, hop down the chimney, distribute the presents under the tree and fill the stockings, eat the cookies and drink milk left by the children, get back up the chimney and back into the sleigh to move to the next house. Very impressive! This works out to 967.7 visits per second.

How fast is Santa's sleigh?

Now that we have calculated how many stops Santa needs to make, it is time to calculate the velocity necessary to reach all the households in less than 36 hours. A third assumption is made in order to make the calculations a lot easier: let's consider that the 482 million homes are evenly distributed around the Earth, so let's say that the distance between each house is around ¾ of a mile. So, Santa approximately travels more than 200 million miles in 35 hours. Therefore, Santa travels around 650 miles per second. This estimate takes into account any emergencies including a quick stop to change out reindeer.

Payload on the sleigh?

The payload on the sleigh adds another interesting element to the computations involving speed and reindeer power. If each child gets nothing more than a medium-sized Lego™ set (2 pounds), the sleigh carries 321,300 tons plus Santa plus the 136,500 tons of coal.

1956. Santa Sliegh at Charles Howard School and Christmas Park, Albion, New York. Photo provided by Phillip Wenz.

How does Santa manage to coordinate with the FAA?

Santa is required to file a flight plan with the FAA every year which is like the International Civil Aviation Organization (ICAO) flight plans. Santa always keeps his flight plan a secret until the last minute. The FAA is always helpful by giving Santa the "right of way" for his flight every Christmas Eve. In NORAD's 58 year history of tracking Santa Claus (Santa's call sign for

Harris & Ewing, photographer. (1927). *Santa Claus receives aeroplane pilot's license from Assistant Secretary of Commerce. Although there may not be sufficient snow for his reindeer sleigh, Santa Claus will still be able to deliver his load of presents on time this Christmas by using the air route. The old saint called at the Commerce Department in Washington today where he is shown receiving an aeroplane pilot's license from Assistant Secretary of Commerce. for Aeronautics William P. MacCracken, while Clarence M. Young (right) Director of Aeronautics, Department of Commerce, looks on. Airway maps and the assurance that the lights would be burning on the airways Christmas Eve were also given to Santa. United States, 1927.* [November] [Photograph] Retrieved from the Library of Congress, https://www.loc.gov/item/2016888549/.

NORAD is "**BIG RED ONE**"), it has continued to innovate and expand its Santa-support mission with the addition of new technology.[46]

In additionally, Santa has been known to use the call sign *"KC25"*. "KC" is for Kris Cringle and "25" is for the date of Christmas. Santa's sleigh four-digit transponder code for the collision avoidance system is *"1225."*

The Gazette. 1955. Sears and Roebuck Ad that led to NORAD Tracking Santa.

In other parts of the world, Santa is assigned additional call signs which alert global aviation administrations, civilian and military, as to Santa's general location. For example, Airservices Australia has designated *"SLEIGH RIDER ONE"* as Santa's call sign over Australian and New Zealand air space and also sends a NOTAM (Notice to Airmen) to warn all other aircraft to stay clear of Santa on December 24th for 36 hours.[47]

What if I want to call Santa?

Sometimes your parents can find a phone number for you to talk to Santa, or at least hear a voice message, but that requires a bit of work since Santa does not always publish his phone number. However, something really extraordinary occurred in December 1955, Sears Roebuck & Co. ran a special advertisement in the Colorado Springs local newspaper, *The Gazette* inviting children to call Santa.

However, the advertisement mistakenly listed the top-secret hotline phone number for Continental Air Defense Command (currently known as North American Aerospace Defense Command (NORAD) which was connected to Director of Operations, Colonel Harry Shoup desk. Colonel Shoup was assigned phone number ME 2-6681.

The organization responsible for protection and tracking of anthing flying over Canada and the United States is NORAD. If you want to follow Santa's journey around the world, children can call the NORAD Command Center starting at 6 a.m. ET on Christmas Eve or check out NORAD's website. The current phone number is:

1-877-HI-NORAD (1-877-446-6723)

NORAD supports Santa using advanced forms of technology to monitor weather and manned aircraft. From a November 27, 2013, statement, NORAD reports:

In the comms [communications] check during the Santa test flight, we learn that the "Intel" [Intelligence] team verified that Jack Frost and Abominable Snowman would not interrupt Santa's important journey on Christmas Eve. The Cyber team ensured that the "anti-Grinch viral" was in place to ensure the nasty green guy doesn't steal Christmas this year via cyber-attack. And other NORAD personnel confirmed their assessment of the "load-bearing capacity for all rooftops that Santa will be landing on."

One of the more interesting tidbits is learning of the upgrades made to ground-based radar systems that can now detect heat signatures from smaller objects in the air, "like the heat generated from Rudolph the Reindeer's red nose."

Why does Santa come down the chimney?

The tradition of Santa Claus entering the homes through the chimney is a long-standing tradition that is based upon the stories of European gift-givers. For instance, Odin from the Norse tradition, Odin would enter through chimneys on the solstice, this event marks the beginning of winter. In Italy, an old woman delivers goodies to kids throughout Italy on Epiphany Eve which is January 5th in the Italian tradition. As Europeans immigrated to North America, the tradition of Santa using the chimney continued.

Many people also believe that Bishop Nicholas started the tradition of coming down the chimney when he tossed the three bags of gold.

Why do children leave cookies and milk for Santa?

Children have always left out food and drink for St. Nicholas to thank him, although some children try to use this to get off the Naughty List. With all the work Santa does on Christmas Eve he gets hungry and thirsty and enjoys this thoughtful gift.

Why do we hang Christmas stockings?

Christmas stockings have been hung by the fire for centuries based on the legend of Saint Nicholas leaving things that the children needed, or money, toys and treats.

Another legend explains why children leave carrots and special food for the reindeer: The Norse god, Odin, would come around and see that children had left food for the reindeer, so he gave them candy and small toys.

What is Mrs. Claus' first name? What does she do?

If you have ever watched movies about Santa Claus, especially *Santa Claus is Coming to Town*, then you know her name is Jessica. She was a schoolteacher who married Kris Kringle, loves to wear red dresses and has a variety of jobs at the North Pole such as looking after the elves and reindeer, taking care of Santa and his special suit, baking cookies and treats and sometimes directs the elf choir.

Candy Canes

According to legend, Christmas candy canes were created in Germany during 1670. The choirmaster at Cologne Cathedral wanted the children to sit through a long Christmas play, so he asked the local candy maker to make candy in the shape of a shepherd's staff in order to remind the children of the shepherds who visited the baby Jesus.

Why do we have Christmas trees?

In ancient days, ornaments that were placed on the Christmas tree were a showcase of symbols for someone to tell a story whether it was a religious story or a personal story. The tree and its decorations were a talking point for the individual and family.

According to many traditions the evergreen fir tree has been used to celebrate winter holidays by both pagans and Christians. It has been widely accepted that the Pagans used the parts of the evergreen tree to decorate their homes for the winter solstice. Christians used the tree to remind them of the everlasting life with God.

Added note in case a child asks about artificial trees: It is perfectly okay to have an artificial tree instead of a live tree! Some children or their parents are allergic to real trees, which means they need to have an artificial tree. Sometimes parents do not have the time to do all the safety precautions needed for live trees, like watering a live tree regularly, so they also use an artificial tree.

Here are some general statistics on live Christmas trees in America:

— The best-known Christmas trees are: Scotch Pine, Douglas Fir, Fraser Fir, Balsam Fir, and White Pine.

— The National Christmas Tree Association has given a Christmas tree to the President and the First Family since 1966.

— Approximately 95 percent of all Christmas trees are grown on Christmas tree farms.

— On average Christmas trees take 6 to 9 years to mature.

— Christmas trees are grown in every state in the United States.

— There are about 2,000 Christmas trees per acre.

— Approximately 80 million Christmas trees are planted each year.

Rockefeller Center. *Skaters and Christmas Tree in 1943.* Library of Congress, Prints & Photographs Division, Gottscho-Schleisner Collection LC-G613-T-44563.

Why such a big tree?

In New York it's not officially Christmastime until the tree is lit at Rockefeller Center. The first tree appeared in 1931 during the Great Depression when workers placed a 20-foot small balsam fir evergreen tree in the dirt of a construction site. That year the tree symbolized Christmas as much as it did hope and the invincible human spirit. The tree was decorated with strings of cranberries, paper garland and a few cans.

Today, the annual Christmas tree at Rockefeller Center is typically adorned with more than 25,000 lights, but no other ornaments except for the 900 pound Swarovski star on top.

Normally the tree average around 80 feet high and 42 feet wide. Sourcing of Christmas tree comes from various Christmas tree farms around the United States. It is a long standing tradition the tree is turned into lumber and donated to Habit for Humanity to help build affordable family homes.

Why would you want spiders in Christmas trees?

To this day, most European cultures believe having a spider or spider web on the Christmas tree is good luck. If you happen to remove or destroy a spider web from your tree, it is considered bad luck.

What can you tell me about Elves?

Elves have been part of the Germanic, British, and Scandinavian folklore and were believed to have magical powers. During the 1800s, Scandinavian writers wrote about Santa's dwarf helpers who kept track of children being naughty or nice and reported their finding back to Santa.

Today, there is no firm number on the elf population at the North Pole. The elves carry out duties such as making and packing toys, tracking the weather, maintaining the naughty-and-nice list, taking care of the reindeer, and maintaining the sleigh.

Reindeer

Before the reindeer can fly anywhere in the world, Santa and the elves need to know all the regulations for each country. Each country must clear the reindeer prior to entry of their airspace. As a condition of entry, the reindeer must be certified by Santa Claus as never having been fed anything other than hay, sugar plums, and gingerbread.

The reindeer must also be individually identified with microchips or official ear-tag identification, and must respond to the names 'Dasher', 'Dancer', 'Prancer', 'Vixen', 'Comet', 'Cupid', 'Donner', 'Blitzen' and 'Rudolph' when interacting with port personnel. No more than one reindeer in the group may be visibly affected by 'Rednose Syndrome', and upon entry, port personnel will visually inspect the reindeer to ensure they are healthy and fit for continued travel. For instance, in the United States, the Department of Agriculture's Animal and Plant Health Inspection Service (APHIS) is required to give them a clean bill of health.

APHIS normally waives disease testing requirements, as the North Pole is recognized by APHIS as a negligible risk for all livestock diseases and at a recent inspection, the reindeer were found to be healthy and able to prance and paw with each hoof.

According to the cheeky release, US port personnel will disinfect the runners and underside of Santa's sleigh once it enters the country. Santa will also have to wash his hands and disinfect his boots. This has been a recurring theme over the past several years.

In the United Kingdom, Santa must follow the 2006 Animal Welfare Act and submit forms such as AML24 — Standard Movement form.

Proper use of "Ho, Ho, Ho"

The use of "Ho" is ineffective as a single gesture. Sometimes saying "Ho Ho" which will have the desired effect on a child or adult. The purpose of "Ho, Ho, Ho" is to garner a smile from the audience and to focus their attention on Santa. Your "Hos" should come from your diaphragm. Overdoing "Ho, Ho, Ho" should be avoided at all costs because then it seems fake. Never say it four times in a row.

Please remember that saying "Ho, Ho, Ho" can sometimes frighten children. For example, in Australia, Santas have been asked NOT to say "Ho, Ho, Ho" but to say "Ha-Ha-Ha" instead because it could be offensive.

Everyone thinks that Santa has the market on "Ho, Ho, Ho" but that's not true. The truth is that "Ho, Ho, Ho" has been used in movies and advertisements other than by Santa. Here are a few examples of the characters from our past who have said "Ho, Ho, Ho":

Jolly Green Giant™
In 1928, the Jolly Green Giant™ character emerged from Grimm's Fairy Tales for his first advertising appearance. He was big and carried a very large pea pod that could resemble the toy sack.

Jabba the Hutt™
Remember "Jabba the Hutt™" from the movie Star Wars™? This large, slug-like alien was the head of the largest criminal empire on the planet of Tatooine.

What is Santa's Zip code?

In the United States of America, children who want to write to Santa may use this address:

If parents inquire how to get a North Pole postmark on a letter, Santa may give out the following:

> North Pole Holiday Postmark
> Postmaster
> 4141 Postmark Drive
> Anchorage AK 99530-9998

Children in Canada can use the zip code HO HO HO to write to Santa. The actual mailing address is:

If you happen to be in France during the Christmas season the children can write a letter (without postage) to Père Noël. Here are the various addresses:

Père Noël au Pôle Nord
33500 Libourne
France

Père Noël au pays des jouets
33500 Libourne
France

Le Père Noël
33500 Libourne
France

Papa Noël au rue des étoiles filantes au ciel
33500 Libourne
France

Christmas Festivals and Traditions

Second Monday in October	Thanksgiving (Canda)
October 31	Halloween
November 1	All Saints Day
November 11	St. Martin's Day (Germany)
Fifth Sunday prior to Christmas	Stir-up Sunday (England)
Fourth Thursday in November	Thanksgiving Day (USA)
December 6	St. Nicholas Day
Fourth Sunday prior to Christmas	Advent begins
December 8	Bohdi Day (Buddhists)
December 10	Hanukah begins (dates varies each year)
December 13	Santa Lucia (Sweden, Italy)
December 15/16	Posados or Novena begins
December 17	Hanukah ends (dates vary each year)
December 19	St. Nicholas Day (Julian Calendar)
December 20/21	St. Ignatius Day (Romania)
December 23	Little Christmas (Demark)
December 24	Christmas Eve
December 25	**Christmas Day**
December 26	St. Stephan (Boxing Day) England; Kwanzaa Day One
December 27	St. John the Evangelist; Mother Night
December 28	Feast of the Holy Victim (Holy Innocents Day)
December 29	St. Thomas Becker/Feast of Fools/Opposite Day
December 30	St. Eqwin of Worcester/Brining of the Bear
December 31	Pope St. Slyvester/St. Basils Day
January 1	The Solemnity of Mary, Mother of Jesus/Snow (News Year Day)
January 2	St. Basil the Great & St. Grefory Nazianzen/Evergreen Day/Holde's Day
January 3	Feast of the Holy Name of Jesus
January 4	St. Elizabeth Ann Seton & St. Simon Stylites/St. Distaff's Day
January 5	St. John Neumann/St. Edward the Confessor (UK) & St. Julian the Hospitaller/Epiphany Eve
January 6	Epiphany, Three Kings Day, Twelfth Night
January 7	Russian Christmas (Julian Calendar)
First Monday after Epiphany	Plough Monday (England)
January 13	Twentieth Day; St. Knut's Day (Scandinavia)
January 19	Tinkat (Ethopia); Epiphany (Julian Calendar)
February 2	Candlemass

Other Nitty Gritty Things Santa Needs to Know

Rules for Santa to Follow

The information listed below is taken from a 1936 memo from Donovan and Shields Department store based in Chicago that was distributed to all their Santas.
Personal Note: I believe that this memo still has relevance today.

1. Bodily Hygiene – As Santa's we must ensure that pay attention to the cleanliness of our suits and our personal appearance.

2. Oral Hygiene – Please don't eat foods that leave an order to your breath before portraying Santa.

3. Fingernails need to be kept short and neat.

4. Trim your Nasal Hairs.

5. Santas must keep their suits, boots and beards clean.

6. Ensure your Santa suit fits properly.

7. Under no circumstances should Santa be intoxicated at any function.

8. No gratuities from the parents when working for the photo company.

9. Should a child become sick on Santa, please excuse yourself politely.

10. Santa should not smoke while in character.

As the times change, so do the rules that Santa needs to perform by. Here are some additional suggested rules to follow:

11. Ensure that your suit and beard is animal fur free; peanut free, tree nut free; legume free; garlic free; dairy free; etc. You could have clients who have severe allergic reaction to these items without you knowing.

12. Never be alone with a child.

13. Never promise a child a gift.

14. Never embarrass anyone.

15. Never make personal remarks about a person's appearance.

16. Never force your beliefs of Santa or religion on others.

17. Never accept a Santa performance you don't feel comfortable about doing. You always need to be able to enjoy what you are doing.

18. Never pass out business cards when you are performing.

19. Never been alone with a single female. Always have your Mrs. Claus, elf, or your sleigh driver go in with you on the visit.

20. Always expect the unexpected.

21. Always be in character when in your costume. Everyone is watching.

22. Always wear white gloves. Never let the wrist be seen.

23. Santa should always keep his hands in plain view. Only touch children in the safe zones.

24. Carry liability insurance for your Santa performances.

25. Carry and stay current on your automobile insurance.

26. Carry a wardrobe kit in your vehicle during the Christmas timeframe.

27. Never collect money at your performance in front of the children. Always collect the payment upfront, in advance of the event if possible.

28. Never talk about another Santa or any business in a negative light.

29. When talking to the media, always consider anything Santa says to be in *print or posted* to social media tomorrow morning.

30. If you accept a performance, make your word count. The family or organization hired you. They want you, not a substitute Santa.

31. Please follow-up with your client the following day, not right at the end of the performance.

32. Be mindful about the parental situation.

33. Never ask what a child would like to receive for Christmas. Santa already knows.

34. Never ask a child if he/she is on the naughty/nice list.

NOTES:

Public Domain versus Copyright

Everyone year Santas around the world take time to read a story to their clients whether it is in the client's home or in a public setting. As Santas, we need to ensure that we are above reproach, and that we adhere to the law. This section will cover the terms "public domain" and "copyright." It is always your responsibility to be certain you check the current rules and regulations. This question always comes up:

Question — Is the poem *'Twas the Night Before Christmas* in public domain?

Answer — The short answer is "yes." The actual original poem is in the public domain. However, if you use a book that was published after 1923 and show the photos or drawings, that is not in public domain. If in doubt, contact the publisher.

Reading Books to the Public

In 2020, many Santas made virtual visits. Surprisingly, the majority of the Santas did not know or understand that when anything is done online a permanent digital file is created on the server you used. For instance, anything broadcasted on Facebook™ remains the property of Facebook™, even after you disable your account.

It is always easier and less costly for you to read a book by contacting the publishing company and requesting permission to read their book. Normally "Gratis Use" policy only applies to public readings where no admission fee is charged to the public.

When submitting the request, always go to the publisher's website and look under "contact us" and "permissions". Normally the following information is required by publishers in order to grant your request:

> Title:
> Author/Illustrator:
> ISBN:
> Date of the reading:
> Location of reading (type of media/distribution):
> Legal name of the requestor:

Then, at your event, remember to do what most publishers require and state the following information before you start reading:

> Title:
> Author/Illustrator:
> Permission was granted by [insert the name of the publisher].

Pay attention to all the rules the publisher wants you to follow, whether the reading is in person or via digital media. This is essential if you want to make this request so you can read an annual item for your Santa business. If your presentation is made by digital media, the publisher or author will require you to delete your reading on digital media by a certain date.

Listed below is the current law provided in an email from the United States Copyright office:

"Generally speaking, in the United States, works first published in the United States or registered with the Copyright Office before 1923 are in the public domain. Works in the public domain no longer have copyright protection and can be freely used without permission. See "Works Published and Copyrighted before January 1, 1978" at https://www.copyright.gov/circs/.

Works first published in the United States with an appropriate copyright notice or registered with the Copyright Office between 1923 to 1963 were initially protected for 28 years. If the copyright for these works was renewed during the 28th year, copyright protection was extended for an additional 67 years. For example, a work published in 1924 may have copyright protection until 2018. For information about copyright renewal, see Circular 15 at https://www.copyright.gov/circs/.

Also, works first published in the United States with an appropriate copyright notice or registered with the Copyright Office between 1964-1977 are automatically renewed and protected for 95 years. For example, a work published in 1964 is protected until 2059. For information about copyright renewal, see Circular 15 at https://www.copyright.gov/circs/.

Furthermore, generally speaking, never published and never registered works created before 1978 and works created after 1977 are generally protected for the life of the author plus 70 years. See "How Long Copyright Protection Endures" on page 5 in Circular 1 Copyright Basics and Circular 15a Duration of Copyright at https://www.copyright.gov/circs/."[53]

Songs

As Santa, you should know the classic songs of the season, especially the songs included in this section which every Santa should know. However, if you perform any of these Christmas songs, you could be liable for performance fees. It is your responsibility to double check whether the song(s) that you use during each of your performances/events is in the Public Domain or is still considered to be under Copyright.

Most children recognize the following songs:

1.   *Rudolph the Red-Nosed Reindeer*
2.   *Santa Claus is coming to Town*
3.   *Deck The Halls*
4.   *Frosty the Snowman*
5.   *Jingle Bells*

The following website can be used to determine which songs are in the public domain or that are copyrighted. https://fairuse.stanford.edu/overview/public-domain/welcome/

Here is a list of copyright and permission terms:

Public Domain refers to creative materials which are not protected by intellectual property laws such as copyright, trademark, or patent laws. The public owns these works, not an individual author or artist. Anyone can use a public domain work without obtaining permission, but no one can ever own it. So, you can feel free to use any of the songs in the Public Domain in your performances/events.

The term ***"Print License to publish the lyrics for songs"*** refers to any songs that are still under copyright and are not considered to be in the Public Domain.

A ***Print License*** is an agreement between a music user and the owner of a copyrighted composition (song), which grants permission to rearrange, print, or display the music notes or lyrics of the song. This permission is also called "print rights." Understand that if you are doing a performance for payment, and use any song not in Public Domain, you could be responsible to pay for a Grand Performance License.

A ***Grand Performance License*** is a type of license which grants you the right to use a piece of music in a play, musical or any other similar performance. You are always responsible to find out if you need a license from the copyright owner in order to use any songs in your portrayal of Santa Claus.

The following songs were in the **public domain** at the time of publication:

Song	Year
Angels from the Realms of Glory	1867
Angels We Have Heard on High	1700
Auld Lang Syne	1711
Away In a Manger	1887
Bring a Torch, Jeanette Isabella	1553
Coventry Carol	Traditional
Deck the Halls	1800
The First Noel	1833
Gesu Bambino	1917
God Rest You Merry, Gentlemen	1827
Go Tell It on the Mountain	1865
Good King Wenceslaus	1853
Hark, the Herald Angels Sing	1840
Here We Come A-Caroling	1850
The Holly and the Ivy	1871
I Heard the Bells on Christmas Day	1872
I Saw Three Ships	1833
In the Bleak Midwinter	Traditional
It Came Upon the Midnight Clear	1850
Jingle Bells	1857
Jolly Old St. Nicholas	1870
Joy to the World	1836
Lo, How a Rose E'er Blooming	1559
O Christmas Tree	1800
O Come All Ye Faithful	1751
O Come, O Come, Emanuel	Traditional
O Holy Night	1847
O Little Town of Bethlehem	1868
Once in Royal David's City	Traditional
Silent Night	1818
Toyland	1903
The Twelve Days of Christmas	1500
Up on the Housetop	1870
The Wassail Song	1600
We Three Kings	1857
We Wish You a Merry Christmas	1500
What Child is This?	1865
While Shepherds Watched	1728

The following songs were under **copyright protection** at the time of publication:

Song	Year
All I Want For Christmas is My Two Front Teeth	(C) 1948
All I Want for Christmas is You	(C) 1994
Blue Christmas	(C) 1964
The Chipmunk Song	(C) 1958
The Christmas Song	(C) 1944
Christmas Time is Here	(C) 1965
The Christmas Waltz	(C) 1954
Do You Hear What I Hear	(C) 1962
Feliz Navidad	(C) 1970
Frosty the Snowman	(C) 1950
Grandma Got Run Over By A Reindeer	(C) 1979
Happy Holiday	(C) 1942
Have Yourself A Merry Little Christmas	(C) 1943
Here Comes Santa Claus	(C) 1947
Holly Jolly Christmas	(C) 1965
Home For The Holidays	(C) 1954
I Saw Mommy Kissing Santa Claus	(C) 1952
I'll Be Home for Christmas	(C) 1943
It's Beginning to Look A Lot Like Christmas	(C) 1951
Jingle Bell Rock	(C) 1957
Last Christmas	(C) 1984
Let It Snow! Let It Snow! Let It Snow!	(C) 1945
The Little Drummer Boy	(C) 1945
Little Saint Nick	(C) 1800
Marshmallow World	(C) 1949
Merry Christmas Darling	(C) 1955
The Most Wonderful Time of The Year	(C) 1963
Rockin' Around The Christmas Tree	(C) 1958
Rudolph, The Red-Nosed Reindeer	(C) 1939
Run Rudolph Run	(C) 1958
Santa Baby	(C) 1953
Santa Claus Is Coming To Town	(C) 1934
Silver Bells	(C) 1950
Sleigh Ride	(C) 1948
Step Into Christmas	(C) 1973
We Need A Little Christmas	(C) 1966
White Christmas	(C) 1940
Winter Wonderland	(C)1934

Names of Santa

From Around the World

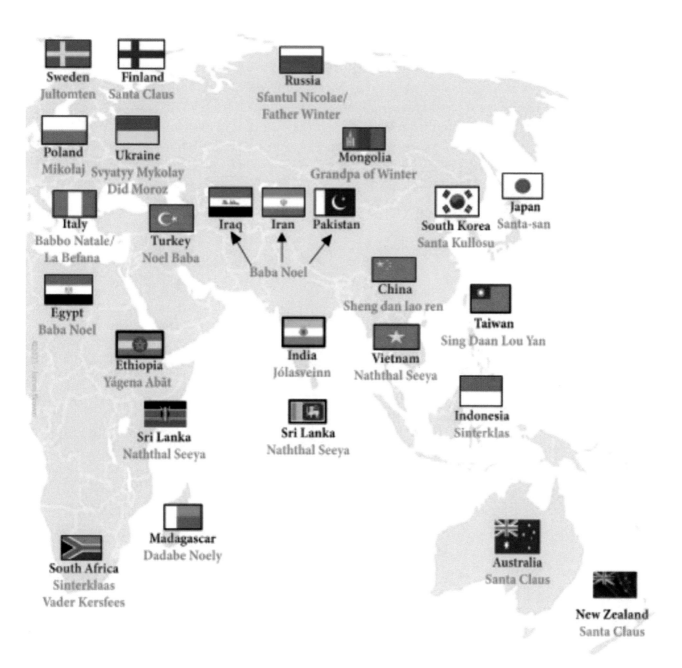

Concluding Thoughts

While there is an almost overwhelming amount of information presented in this chapter, please understand that it is here to help you to portray Santa. Having a practiced response to questions frequently asked, along with solid background details on major points like the reindeer, helps you engage smoothly with clients and builds confidence. Also, understanding the nitty gritty about public domain versus copyright is essential to avoid any mishaps with your events and with your business. As Santa, you are responsible for what you share with children and clients. Enjoy learning what might seem like trivia to you, but is highly likely to be an earth-shattering, need-to-know question for a child. Remember that all the behind-the-scenes preparation allows Santa to create a magical experience for one and all!

And Finally.......

How to End Your Career as Santa

As we all approach our "Golden Reward" aka retirement, we must be honest and upfront with ourselves and our families. Being Santa is a very rewarding job but also very stressful. As we continuously grow older our bodies take stress differently and we learn that we have additional limitations such as driving at night. We are often reminded that a good Santa professional lifespan in this business is only 5-10 years because of our age and health.

One must truly ask himself is it time to allow someone else take the reins of the sleigh. If so, have you taken the time to properly prepare the next Santa to take over and care for your current clients? These are the questions you should ask yourself.

I am in the middle of writing down everything that I have learned from the other Santas around me including what not to do. Santas should be willing to share the tradecraft in order to keep the *"Spirit of Christmas"* alive.

After you have considered your thoughts, talk to your Mrs. Claus or your family about your decision; get their input. See if they are willing to help you with your Santa visits such as driving at night, scheduling your visits, and helping during the visit. If they are unable to do so or if they know that you need to step aside, please listen to the voice of reason. They are your family. Most of the time, your family has your best interest at heart.

If you are passing the reins, help your clients find someone that will fill your boots and keep the *"Spirit of Christmas"* alive. As I finish this section today, we recently had a Santa pass away in a nearby community. He had a large number of clients who are scrambling to find a replacement Santa. They want to find a replacement without having to check out the Santa before they hire their new Santa. Please do the right thing.

Wishing you a very Merry Christmas and a successful career!

So now you have as much information and tips on establishing your Santa business as could be squeezed into this book: Essential things to consider in starting up, running the business, working with people of all ages/abilities and even how to end your Santa career. Remember that this book should be used as a guide, since there will always be new strategies and technologies. Having a Santa who will serve as your mentor would be priceless, just as my own Santa mentor has been to me. This has been quite the adventure with countless hours searching for detailed history and for experts on essential things such as the Beard chapter and merging that all in with my personal experiences. But above everything else, being Santa has been a deep source of joy for me which I share with my clients, and I hope I have been able to share it with you. May you find this book helpful and may it lead you to a place where you board your own sleigh, calling out "Ho, Ho, Ho!"

Appendix

Let us have music for Christmas...
Sound the trumpt of joy and rebirth;
Let each of us try, with a song in our hearts.
To bring peace to men on Earth.
- Mildred L. Jarrell

Appendix A
How to Set Up Social Media Accounts & Related Definitions

Directions to set up Facebook™ account

How to set up a Facebook™ Page for your business:

Step 1 – Sign up. Go to facebook.com/business and click "Create a Page." Then decide on your type of business.

Step 2 – Add pictures. Decide on a profile picture and a cover photo for your business.

Step 3 – Explore your new Page

Step 4 – Add a short description. Click on Add a Short Description, then share with your customers a clear and concise business statement.

Step 5 – Create your username. Make your username your stage name as Santa. Use the name you use on your business cards and your website.

Step 6 – Complete your business section. This is the business information section of your page to provide relevant content about your business.

Step 7 – Create your first post. Provide valuable information for your first business post.

Step 8 – Post items only relevant to your business. Keep your personal, religious, and political posts off your business page.

How to set-up an Instagram™ Account

Step 1 – Download and launch the app. Open it once it has been downloaded.

Step 2 – Click on "Sign up" and enter your email address or phone number to register. Alternatively, tap "Sign in" with Facebook. Choose your username and complete the registration. Then, sign into the Instagram app on your mobile device.

Step 3 – Go to the main page and visit your profile (main page). Find the button "Switch to Business Profile" option in the "Settings" list menu.

Step 4 – Click on "Continue" until you arrive at the "Connect the Facebook™ Page" screen.

Step 5 – Find the Facebook™ Page of your business in order to link it to your Instagram™ profile. (***Note:*** As the administrator, you will only see the pages that are connected with Instagram™ and Facebook™.

Step 6 – Take the time to fill out your profile page. This will provide information to your customers.

Step 7 – Click away.

Login Name:
Password:

Twitter™

One of the first things you can do is to study the home page. Learn the homepage and learn where your account information is located which needs to be filled out. Here are the steps to set up the account, along with definitions of frequently used terms.

1. How to set-up a Twitter™ Account

    a. Open a Twitter™ account. Go to https://www.twitter.com/ in your computer's web browser.
    b. Click on sign up (the blue button) on the right side of the page.
    c. Create a name for your account
    d. Add your phone number.
    e. Click on "next"
    f. Read Terms of Service and then click "Sign up"
    g. Use the verification code into the box that was sent to your registered phone.
    h. Enter a password once your verification code has been accepted.
    i. Click next.
    j. Verify your email address if you signed up with an email address
    k. Upload a profile photo
    l. Select people to follow.

2. Setting up your profile.

    a. Click on your profile icon. You will see a drop-down menu to make choices from in order to update your account.
    b. Click on "Settings and privacy". This is the settings page.
    c. Click on username box and replace the generated name with your replacement name.

     d.   Save your changes.
     e.   Enter your password when prompted.
     f.   Click save changes.
     g.   Click on the profile picture icon
     h.   Upload your photo
     i.   Fill out your profile information
     j.   Select a theme color.

3. How to Tweet

     a.   Click on Tweet. (Top right corner)
     b.   Enter your tweets text. You have up to 280 characters
     c.   Add a photo to your tweet.
           i.   Click on the "Photo Icon."
           ii.   Select a photo or video from your device.
           iii.   Click "open."
     d.   Animated photo than a regular photo
           i.   Click on the GIF button below the tweet box.
           ii.   Select GIF category.
           iii.   Upload GIF.
     e.   Create a "Poll" on Twitter™.
           i.   Click on Tweet, and your question to the text box
           ii.   Click on bar graph-shaped "Poll" icon.
           iii.   Add poll choices in the "Choice 1" and "Choice 2" text fields. You can add more by click Add a choice.
           iv.   You can set a time limit. Maximum limit is 7 days.
           v.   Click Tweet.

Twitter™ Definitions

Twitter™ — an online social networking platform that allows users to send and receive text-based message, or "tweets."

Tweets — text-based messages of up to 140 characters (letters, symbols, words, spaces, and punctuation.)

@ — a way of referring to another user, for example, my username is @Santa

Twitter™ Feed — the running list of tweets

RT — A retweet– or RT—when you share the tweet of another user with all of your Twitter followers.

MT — a modified retweet—or MT—that's been modified or edited in some way

Reply — when you directly respond to a specific user beginning with their username

DM — direct message. You can only direct message someone you follow.

Follower — Someone who follows YOU on Twitter™. On Twitter™ you don't have to follow your followers in order to make communication work.

Hashtags — A hashtag (#) is a word or phrase preceded by a "#." By using hashtags, you can aggregate tweets around that topic. Hashtags (#) helps keep the discussion on a specific topic. You may add a # (hashtag) to any tweet.

Google My Business™

In order to use this feature, you will need to create a Business Profile on Google™. Simply go to https://www.google.com/business/ and follow the provided directions.

You can provide the following information for your business profile:

1. Business name
2. Phone number
3. Website/Facebook page
4. Email address
5. Hours
6. Address if you have a permanent storefront.
7. Photos
8. Description of your business

YouTube™

Here are simple instructions to create a business account.

1. First create your account.
2. Once you have signed in, go to your channel list tab.
3. Choose to create a new channel and click on Create a new channel.
4. Fill out the details to name your new channel and verify your account. Then, click Done. This creates a new business account.
5. To add a channel manager, follow the instructions to change channel owners and managers.

Appendix B
Mrs. Claus Outfit

For those of you who have a partner willing and desiring to portray Mrs. Claus, here is some information to help you get started. A few basic facts about Mrs. Claus will also assist in developing the personality/character: Her first name is Jessica and she has a knack for baking and matching toys with children on the Nice List.

Basic Mrs. Claus Outfit Cost Breakdown

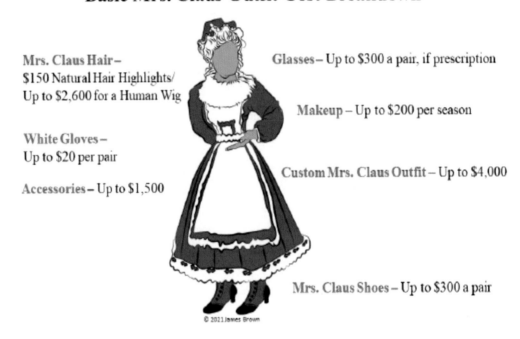

Mrs. Claus Hair – $150 Natural Hair Highlights/ Up to $2,600 for a Human Wig

White Gloves – Up to $20 per pair

Accessories – Up to $1,500

Glasses – Up to $300 a pair, if prescription

Makeup – Up to $200 per season

Custom Mrs. Claus Outfit – Up to $4,000

Mrs. Claus Shoes – Up to $300 a pair

© 2021 James Brown

Buying an Off-the-Rack Outfit
If you don't want to assemble a costume or make your own look, you can purchase a Mrs. Claus costume ready-made. This is an easy option, perfect if you're short on time. A pre-bought Mrs. Claus that is available in women's sizes up to extra-large retails for about $136.

Additional Looks for Your Mrs. Claus Outfit
It is easy to make high-end adjustments to your Mrs. Claus outfit without the need of spending lots of money. A simple trip to your local thrift store can yield sweaters, skirts, or dresses which can be easily modified for your use. You can always add white fur onto the hems and cuffs of the outfits and some white glitter fabric paint or glitter glue for a sparkly touch. An inexpensive bracelet and earrings, along with fun white or holiday tights can also add fun and magic to Mrs. Claus' look.

Shoes for Mrs. Claus

Since Mrs. Claus seems to be on her feet most of the time, greeting clients and helping with refreshments, having comfortable shoes is a necessity. Be sure to have shoes which fit well, are easy to clean and support your ankles and arches! There are so many options to complete your Mrs. Claus look: ankle boots, calf-high boots, Mary Jane style shoes, flats or even white or black running shoes. Let your personality influence your selection.

Creating Your Own Mrs. Claus Outfit

For those who would prefer to make their own Mrs. Claus outfit, here is some information for you.

Most fabric stores carry patterns to make such outfits. The most traditional patterns are **McCall's M5550 Santa Claus Christmas Costume Sewing Pattern** and **Simplicity Pattern 2542 Adult Costumes**. Both patterns will need slight alterations to fit your needs. You will need about a month's lead time to make the outfit before the big Christmas season push.

Type of Fabric need	Quantity
Red Felt Fabric	2 yards of 60 inch wide
Red Satin Ribbon	0.5 yards
White Fur Trim	5 1/2 Yards

In addition, for the Mrs. Claus apron you could use **McCall's M2233**, **M5284**, or **M7208**. An apron will run approximately 2 yards of fabric plus ribbon and any additional accessories.

McCall's pattern M2233 contains both a bonnet and apron pattern. This pattern is an older version of the bonnet.

You can have fun with the apron and headwear fabric, creating contrasting looks or using patterned fabric (gingerbread, reindeer, snowflakes, etc.). Be sure to pick up a little extra of the fabric in case you want to add things like handkerchiefs, or to have on hand in case you make any mistakes.

Custom - Made Mrs. Claus Outfit Measurements

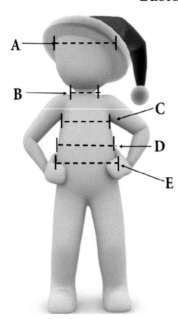

A – Head measurements

Measure the circumference of the head at mid-brow level; just above the ears & eyebrows. If a wig is worn, include it in the measurement. (do not wear a hat). Do you wear a wig? Yes   No   If so, take measurements of including wig in inches/centimeters: ——

B – Neckline Measurements:

Measure the circumference of the neck at its base. Please provide measurements in inches/centimeters: ————————

C – Bust Measurements:

Measure the circumference of the bust, please provide measurements in inches/centimeters: ————————

D – Natural Waist Measurements:

Measure the circumference of your natural waist in inches/ centimeters: ————————

E – Natural Hip Measurements:

Measure the circumference of your natural hips in inches/centimeters: ————————

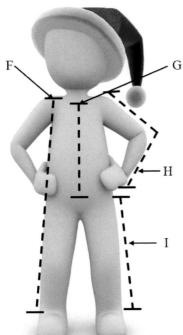

F – Robe:

Measure from the base of the neck to the heel. Please provide measurement in inches/centimeters: ————————

G – Coat:

Measure the middle of the back from the base of the neck to the top of leg. Please provide inches/centimeters: ————————

H – Sleeve Length:

Continuing from "Top Shoulder," measure from the very top of the arm, where it meets the edge of the shoulder, to the base of the wrist, with elbow bent and forearm at a 90-degree angle in front of the body. If so, take measurements of including wig in inches/centimeters: ————————

I – Outer seam:

Measure the outer leg from the waistline to the top of the foot; knicker-style pants cling to the ankle with elastic and are made to blouse over mid-calf boots. Please provide measurements in inches/centimeters:————————

B-3

Mrs. Claus Hair (Wig)

If you are going for this classic traditional look, you will need to have white hair. Mrs. Claus hair comes in different colors depending on your choice. You will need to figure out which you prefer:

Mrs. Claus wig (Please see the section on Wigs and Beards)
Bleaching your hair white
Your hair is already white
Keeping your hair your natural color.

Wire-Rimmed Glasses

Mrs. Claus' glasses come in many shapes and designs. However, the American public associates Mrs. Claus with golden round glasses.

As with Santa's glasses, if you do not usually wear glasses or if you use contacts, then you can purchase non-prescription glasses for much less money than if you need/choose to obtain prescription glasses in this style.

White Gloves

Again, just like Santa, Mrs. Claus should opt for white gloves especially when around younger clients. This color blends well with the outfit and shows up well on pictures, which can protect both you and the client from any mishaps. Gloves should fit well, be clean and cover any tattoos.

Make-up

While you are likely very familiar with make-up, you may need to check in with a make-up artist or use Google to find tips on making your make-up last for an event, to avoid problems if you tend to sweat. You do not want to get make-up onto your hair/wig or bonnet and gloves during the event. You will want to ensure you have extra supplies on hand for emergencies or touch-ups. Read back through the section in the book on make-up for more suggestions on how to develop your Mrs. Claus look.

Appendix C
Beard Care/Styling Directions

Caring for your Beard

Required items:
>Beard shampoo or soap
>Beard conditioner
>Trimming scissors

Step 1 — Wash your beard, just like the way you wash your hair with shampoo and warm water.

Step 2 — Gently pat and wipe your beard dry with a towel after washing.

Step 3 — Use conditioner to add a little shine.

Step 4 — Keep the dead ends trimmed off your beard.

Styling Your Beard

Required items:
>Hand towel
>Beard comb and styling brush
>Blow dryer
>Curling iron and/or hot rollers
>Unscented hairspray

Step 1 — Towel dry your beard first, leaving the hair damp. Then use your fingers to comb out the beard, followed by combing again with the wide tooth comb.

Step 2 — Blow dry the beard into place. Use it to shape your beard while it is damp, not soaking wet. Instead, work upwards from your neck and dry out the beard. You may need to use the brush to hold hair in place as you blow dry. It'll puff out so it looks nice and full. Blow it down so it falls into the basic shape you desire.

Step 3 — Comb or brush out the beard to finish styling it. Work slowly, pulling the comb through your hair. Finish off your style by brushing out the hair. Combs are great for styling small areas and details. Brushes can smooth out larger areas in a shorter amount of time. It's up to you to decide which options work best for you.

Step 4 —You may use a curling iron or hot rollers to finish styling your beard. If you desire to add a curl to your beard, wind the beard hairs in rollers and let them set for 20-25 minutes and then remove. If the hair starts to fray or frizz, comb it out gently. Then spray with non-scented hairspray. In case you have never used hairspray, be sure to keep your mouth closed and do not breathe while spraying.

Grooming Real Mustaches

If you lack experience with styling mustaches, either check with a hair stylist or possibly with other Santas or mustache/beard groups, to get tips on how to do this.

Required items:
       Beard/mustache comb and styling brush
       Hair dryer
       Curling iron – mini sized
       Mustache/beard wax
       Needle-nosed pliers

Step 1 — While your mustache is wet, comb your mustache in a down direction.

Step 2 — Take your hair dryer and brush, curl the mustache in the down direction. Then take the brush around the end of mustache and curl in an upward motion.

Step 3 — Take mustache wax (beard wax) and wax it into your mustache.

Step 4 — Twist your mustached to create the handlebar shape.

Step 5 — Take your hairdryer with a pair of needle nose pliers to hold your mustache in place while the hairdryer melts the wax to create a stiff mustache.

Step 6 — Once the mustache is in place, cool your mustache down as quickly as possible so the wax "freezes" in place.

Appendix D
Color & Bleach At Home Directions

Coloring Santa's Hair at Home

Always before you attempt to color your own hair, speak to a hair care professional first. If you have any doubts about bleaching and/or colori your own hair, call the number on the box of hair dye first before trying this on your own.

Note: The following includes general information and is not intended to replace advice and suggestions from a hair care professional. The author is not liable for any mishaps or injuries occurring from coloring or bleaching.

Step 1 — Select a Color
At the time of writing this section, the current literature recommends staying within one or two shades of your natural hue. Don't go by the model on the box. Your results will be different than the model's results. Check the side of the box for a more accurate indicator of what your hair will look like.

Step 2 — Condition Your Hair
Before coloring your hair, you want to do a deep conditioning of your hair two days prior to your treatment to help strengthen hair. Then wash your hair the night before you're going to color, not on the same day. If you wash your hair the day of your treatment, you could cause an abrasive to your skin caused by your fingernails.

Step 3 — Prep the Bathroom. Here are the essentials to ensure you can do your own coloring:

1. Wide-tooth comb
2. Four large hair clips
3. Kitchen timer
4. Jar of petroleum jelly – Apply the jelly along your hairline to protect your skin from staining
5. Old button-down shirt
6. Gloves
7. Shampoo and conditioner designed for colored/bleached hair

Step 4 — Read the Instructions
Always read and follow the instructions. You will find different manufactures have different steps for you to do as you color your hair. Again: Read the directions carefully, follow instructions and call the dye company with any questions.

Step 5 — Divide & Conquer

A. Using the comb, divide dry hair into four sections: down the middle, then across the center from side to side. Twist and clip each section.

B. Starting with a front section, unclip hair and apply color along the roots.

C. With your gloved fingers, gently run color from roots to ends. Repeat on each section.

Step 6 — Set a Timer
Once you've finished applying color to your last section of hair, start a timer for the specific amount of time as stated on the box. Follow the instructions on the box.

Step 7 — Rinse and Shine
Once the timer rings, begin the process according to the instructions on the box on how to rinse and shampoo after coloring. Most coloring kits will recommend which shampoo and conditioner to use or may even include it in the box.

Finally, please remember, hair looks different wet than dry, so always dry your hair after coloring to see the final shade. If for some reason you did not get the results you were expecting and you are unhappy with the result, don't panic! Call the toll-free number on the box and talk to a hair color expert who can help you fix the problem. These people are trained to help you overcome the issue. For example, if some of your gray is still showing, they may recommend you shampoo your hair and do a touchup application 48 hours later.

Be proactive: Call and speak to a hair color expert before coloring to get extra tips on applying that specific kit. You may decide to go with having a professional hair stylist do the bleaching and/or coloring for you instead of doing this at home.

Appendix E
Sign Language

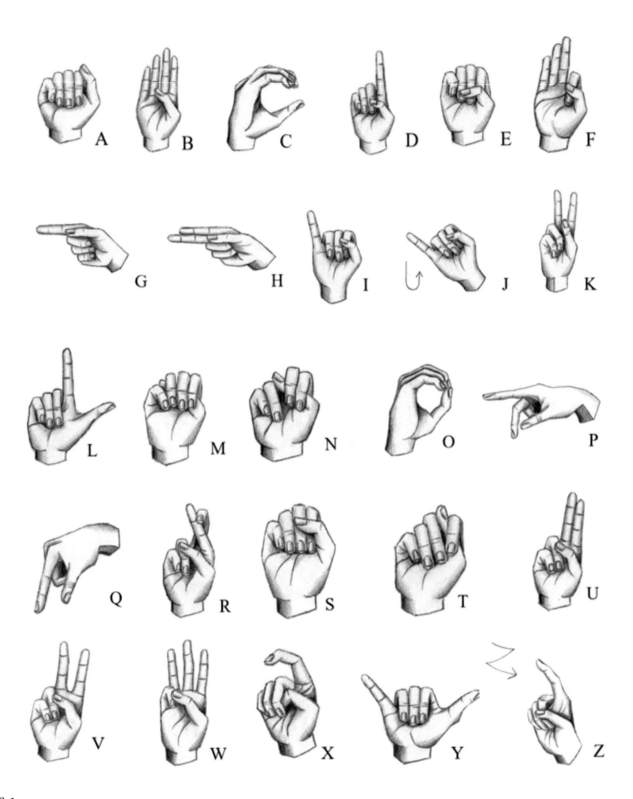

Sign Language - Numbers

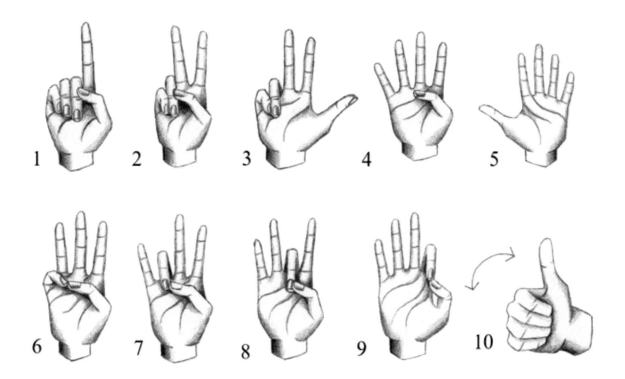

Commonly Used Christmas Words

Angel – Form the hands with the fingers held together and straight. Tap the fingertips to the shoulders with the palms facing down. Lift and twist the hands around with the palms facing forward. The sign for angel resembles angel wings.

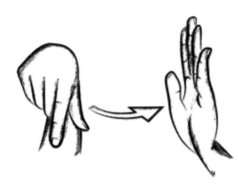

Bells – You take your non-dominant hand open and stand your whole forearm up as if to make the wall of a bell. Then you take your dominant hand in a first, with thumb and index finger both pointing down.

Bethlehem – Sign the letter B of the sign language alphabet in front of the chin. Form the letter B with both hands. Touch the fingertips of the hands together to form an upside-down V on the left side of the body. Then touch the fingertips of the hands together to form an upside-down V in the center of the body.

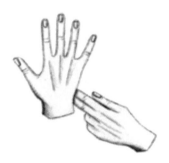

Candle – Hold up your dominant hand vertically with fingers pointing up towards the sky. Point your index finger from your non-dominant hand to the base of the palm of your dominant hand. Then wiggle the fingers of your dominant hand.

Christmas – Hold the left arm in front of the body across the chest with the palm facing down. Rest the elbow of the right arm on top of the back of the left hand. Form the right hand into the shape of the letter C. Place the right hand on the left elbow. Lift the right arm from the elbow in an arching motion in front of the body.

Cookies – Use your dominant hand is in a loose "C" handshape. You bring that hand down onto the opposite hand, then lift it back up while rotating it rotate it and bring it down again on the hand. Twist your hand as if cutting out cookies from cookie dough.

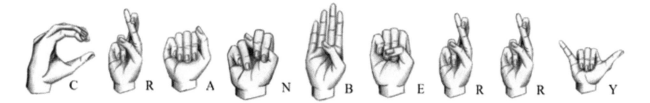

Cranberry – Fingerspell the word C-R-A-N-B-E-R-R-Y with the sign language alphabet.

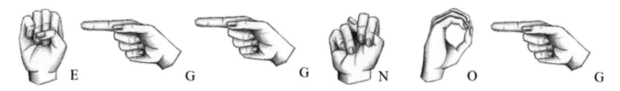

Eggnog – Fingerspell the word E-G-G-N-O-G with the sign language alphabet.

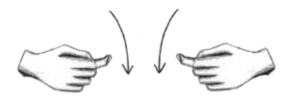

Gifts/presents – Form the letter X of the sign language alphabet with both hands. Hold both hands in front of the body at waist level. Move both hands forward twice.

H O   H O   H O

HO, HO, HO

I   V   Y

Ivy – Fingerspell the word I-V-Y with the sign language alphabet.

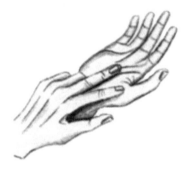

Jesus – Hold both hands in front of the chest with the right palm facing left and the left palm facing right. Tap the middle finger of the right hand to the left palm. Then tap the middle finger of the left hand to the right palm.

Mistletoe – Form a squished letter X of the sign language alphabet with the right hand. Hold the right hand above the head. Form the number 2 in sign language with the left hand. Touch the tips of the left index and middle fingers to the right side of the mouth. Slide the left fingertips to the middle of the cheek. The sign for mistletoe resembles receiving a kiss under the mistletoe.

Ornament – Form a flattened letter "O" of the sign language alphabet with both hands. Touch the fingertips together. Hold the hands in front of the chin. Twist the fingertips together three times while moving the hands to the right.

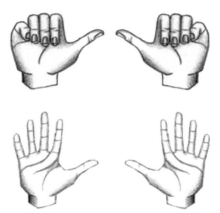

Reindeer – Form the number 5 in sign language with both hands. Tap the thumbs to the temples of the forehead with the palms facing forward twice. The sign for reindeer resembles reindeer antlers.

Mrs. Santa Claus

Santa Claus – Form the number 5 in sign language with both hands and curl the fingers and thumbs in to form half circles. Place the hands at the chin. Make two half circles with the hands while moving the hands down from the chin. The sign for Santa Claus resembles a beard.

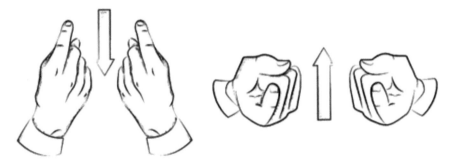

Sleigh – Form the letter V of the sign language alphabet with both hands. Begin with the hands in front of the shoulders. Move both hands down at an angle while bending the index and middle fingers. The sign for sleigh resembles the runners on a sleigh.

Snow – Form the number 5 in sign language with both hands. Begin with the hands on either side of the face. Lower the hands to the waist while wiggling the fingers.

Star – Form the number 1 in sign language with both hands. Hold the hands in front of the chin with the palms facing forward and the index fingers pointing up. Bounce the fingers up and down.

T   I   N   S   E   L

Tinsel – Fingerspell the word T-I-N-S-E-L with the sign language alphabet.

T

Toy – Make your two hands into a fist and tuck your thumb up between your index finger and middle finger on each hand. Twist your hands back and forth to make the sign.

Tree – Hold the left arm in front of the body at waist level with the palm facing down. Place the right elbow on top of the left hand and hold the right arm straight up. Hold the fingers of the right hand apart and twist the right wrist back and forth.

Appendix F
Spanish Words for Christmas

With the ever-increasing Spanish populations in the United States, it has become more important than ever to learn Spanish words for the Christmas season. We have listed the most common words and phrases.

Christmas Greetings

Wishing someone Merry Christmas in Spanish. Here are some common Christmas greetings and well wishes:

¡Feliz Navidad! - Merry Christmas!
¡Felices fiestas! - Happy holidays!
¡Feliz Navidad y próspero Año Nuevo! - Merry Christmas and a happy New Year!
Que pases lindo esta Navidad. - Have a nice time this Christmas.
¡Te deseo una feliz Navidad! - I wish you a Merry Christmas!
¡Mis mejores deseos para esta Navidad! - All my best wishes for this Christmas!
Brindo por - I toast to...
La familia - Family
Los amigos - Friends

Christmas Holidays

La Navidad - Christmas
La Nochebuena - Christmas Eve
El día de Navidad - Christmas Day
La medianoche - Midnight

Decorations

El árbol/arbolito de Navidad - Christmas tree
Los adornos - Decorations
La guirnalda - Garland
El muérdago - Mistletoe
Las luces - Lights

Food & Drink

El turrón - Nougat (a common food around Christmas time in most Spanish-speaking countries)
El mazapán - Marzipan
Las galletas/galletitas - Cookies
Los frutos secos - A general term for nuts, almonds and the like.

El panettone/El pan dulce - Panettone
El lechón - A pork-based dish, a young pig.
El pavo - Turkey
El cordero - Lamb
El champán - Champagne
El vino - Wine
La sidra - Cider

Other Traditions

Los regalos - Presents
Abrir los regalos - Open the presents
La cena - Dinner
Comer -To eat
Brindar - To make a toast
El brindis - Toast
La fiesta - Party
Papá Noel/San Nicolás - Santa Claus
El trineo - Sleigh
Los renos - Reindeer
El villancico - Christmas carol
La tarjeta - Card

Christmas Religious Terms

¡Que Dios te bendiga! - May God bless you!
El niño Jesús - Baby Jesus
La virgen María - Virgin Mary
La iglesia - Church
La misa - Mass
La Misa de Gallo - A Christmas mass held around midnight.
¿A qué hora es la misa? - At what time is mass held?
¿Dónde es la misa? - Where is mass held?
El belén/pesebre - Nativity scene

Spanish Phrases

¿Como te yamas? What is your name?
¿Qué quieres para Navidad? What do you want for Christmas?
¿Has sido una chica buena (girl)? Have you been a good girl?
¿Has sido un chico bueno? Have you been a good boy?
Sonríe para la cámara. Smile for the camera.
¿Te gustaría un dulce? Would you like some candy?

Appendix G:
Portraying Mrs. Claus

Christmas is about love and family. Thus, for most of us, when you think of Christmas, you think of a family event which includes a married couple. Santa and Mrs. Claus make the perfect nostalgic couple, especially when they arrive at an event together. The host often says the mood of the event normally changes to become more of a family function.

Now Santa, everyone knows that you are a gentleman and that you will treat Mrs. Claus with respect. Even so, Santa, you have young men watching how you treat a lady. You will etch memories in the child's mind. Take advantage of it and show some chivalry. Be a role model for young men of how to properly act towards and around young ladies.

Yes, Mrs. Claus, please allow Santa to treat you like a queen which includes opening the car door for you, helping you with your jacket and escorting you into the event. You will have young ladies watching how Santa treats you like royalty. Accept Santa's help graciously, understanding you are not exhibiting weakness, but rather demonstrating for the young ladies how to give young men an opportunity to show their respect.

Prior to arriving, both Santa and Mrs. Claus need to ensure that they have the same backstory on their lives together. Mrs. Claus can expect to receive the bulk of the questions from the young ladies. Some of those questions could be: Where did you meet Santa? What is Santa's favorite toy? What is his favorite game to play? What is Santa's favorite cookie? Ensure you know the answers because children will go and ask Santa the same questions about himself to check that the answers are the same.

Santa, ensure that you know the answers the above questions in regard to Mrs. Claus. Don't be surprised if the children go and check the answers out on the internet.

When Mrs. Claus works with Santa Claus, Mr. Claus needs to understand that she is there as his equal. The two of you need to operate as a team, able to move in and support each other as different situations arise. Mrs. Claus' duties while attending an event with Santa will vary depending on the visit. Engaging with event guests and children, reading, or telling stories, helping with cookies or games, and more are all part of what any Mrs. Claus might do in portraying Mrs. Claus.

Rest assured: Mrs. Claus brings with her a certain finesse that can enhance the Christmas visit. Mrs. Claus is able to "work" the party by boosting the level of trust between Santa and the children. When Mrs. Claus is at the party with Mr. Claus, her duty is to ensure that she bridges the gap between the children and Santa by being the intermediator of the two groups. She is Santa's equal.

Mrs. Claus needs to feel comfortable in her outfit, hair, and makeup. According to a podcast of Deanna Golden on The Professional Santa Claus' Podcast, "Mrs. Claus needs to dress for the event she is attending." So, if you are attending a cookie decorating session, have an apron. If you are attending a party, dress up a bit more for the party.

Events that Mrs. Claus normally attends:

- Amusement Parks
- Decorating Cookies
- Entertaining children at various home events
- Fund raising activities
- Nursing Homes/Memory Care Homes
- Mall events
- Parades with Santa Claus
- Photography with Santa and Mrs. Claus or just with Mrs. Claus
- Preschools/Elementary Schools
- Resorts
- Storytime
- Tea Parties

Mrs. Claus Outfit and Accessories

Mrs. Claus has the ability to set the tone for any event she attends. Dress for the occasion. Santa is bound by the "red suit." However, society has given Mrs. Claus the ability to change her attire to match the event she will be attending.

As most of us know and have seen in some format, Santa carries a bunch of keys on his belt. I bet Mrs. Claus has her own set of keys just like Santa, which very likely are for:

Classroom Key: Mrs. Claus (known as Jessica) was responsible for education in Sombertown before she married Kris Kringle. Since she had experience, it was only fitting that she would be responsible for the education at the North Pole as the school's headmaster.

Reindeer Barn Key: Mrs. Claus has reindeer which pull her sleigh for errands.

Greenhouse Key: Mrs. Claus does enjoy gardening and uses fresh organic ingredients whenever possible.

Tea Room Key: Mrs. Claus does drink tea. She probably has tea parties a couple times a year, enjoying the delicious treats she makes with the tea. SECRET hot chocolate recipe. Mrs. Claus has Santa's hot chocolate available to classified locations around the world.

Medical Supplies Key: Mrs. Claus supervises the healthcare for the North Pole Elves and Santa.

Gift Wrapping Department Key: For those who shop for wrapping paper each year, you may have noticed last year's paper is not available this year. Mrs. Claus is in charge of providing the latest types of wrapping each year. She probably has a team of elves that does market research on the current trends around the world and targets certain consumer markets with different types of wrapping paper.

Cookie Department Key: Mrs. Claus oversees the development of cookie recipes used around the world. We all know and understand that Santa loves the chocolate chip cookie developed by Toll House™.

Hot Chocolate Department Key: Mrs. Claus ensures the protection of Santa's TOP SE-CRET hot chocolate recipe. Mrs. Claus has Santa's hot chocolate available to classified locations around the world.

Tailor Shop Key: Mrs. Claus is responsible to ensure Santa's suit is ready to go for the big night (aka Christmas Eve). This is a top priority!

Music and Choir Room Key: In *Rudolph the Red-Nose Reindeer*, Mrs. Claus is shown directing the choir. This is something you might see her do when visiting with children at various parties since she can direct humans as well as elves.

Portraying Mrs. Claus requires a balance of creativity, love of children and organization. To be Mrs. Claus, you also need to be prepared to dress the part. Having a "day" dress for informal or baking/decorating occasions and a special cape to wear for more formal events, or a woolen cape for outdoor events, along with comfortable shoes is all essential. Keep your make up from being too glamorous or "clowny" – be natural and match Santa with the rosy cheeks. Even the more modern portrayers of Mrs. Claus tend to keep with white hair, although the styling could be more individualized. Most of all, however, please keep in mind that while you are indeed equal to Santa, your primary role is to work with Santa as a teammate. Enjoy your time as Mrs. Claus!

Endnotes

Setting up Your Santa Business

1 Clark, T. L. (2017, December 22). *Santa's taxes and other seasonal jobs: H&R Block Newsroom*. Retrieved January 28, 2020, from https://www.hrblock.com/tax-center/newsroom/ income/heres-santa-theres-santa-everywhere-theres-santa-whats-real-deal-santas-taxes/.

Taxes

2 INTUIT, Inc. (1992). Washington, DC: U.S. Patent and Trademark Office.

3 Entertainment Audit Technique Guide. Internal Revenue Service - Entertainment Audit Technique Guide. (2015). https://www.irs.gov/businesses/small-businesses-self-employed/audit-techniques-guides-atgs.

4 Clark, T. L. (2017, December 22). Santa's taxes and other seasonal jobs: H&R Block Newsroom. Retrieved January 28, 2020, from https://www.hrblock.com/tax-center/newsroom/ income/heres-santa-theres-santa-everywhere-theres-santa-whats-real-deal-santas-taxes/.

Background Check

5 Talley, J. (2012, December 19). Whose Lap Is That, Anyway? Mall Santa Background Checks. Retrieved March 15, 2020, from https://stories.avvo.com/crime/whoselap.html.

Social Media Background Checks

6 Lozier, T. (2019, December 3). Conducting Social Media Background Checks Before Hiring. Valiant. Retrieved September 12, 2021, from https://www.valiant.com/conducting-social-media-background-checks-before-hiring

7 Ways One Can Fail a Social Media Background Check? Crimcheck. (2021, February 1). Retrieved September 12, 2021, from https://crimcheck.net/news/9-ways-to-fail-a-social-media-background-check/.

Liability Insurance

8 Ramsey Solutions. (2019, July 8). Basic Insurance Policies Everyone Needs. Retrieved January 28, 2020, from https://www.daveramsey.com/blog/basic-insurance-policies-everyone-needs.

9 ICSC Forecasts 3.3 Percent Growth this Holiday Season Source-. (2016, October 4). Retrieved November 15, 2018, from https://www.icsc.org/news-and-views/icsc-exchange/icsc-forecasts-33-percent-growth-this-holiday-season.

10 Anderson, W. (2013, December 3) Five Things You Might Not Know About Mall Santas. Retrieved November 15, 2018, from https://www.huffingtonpost.ca/ward-anderson/mall-santasb4357353.html

Free Lance Santa

11 Federal Trade Commission. (2017, December 15). Price Fixing. Retrieved October 05, 2020, from https://www.ftc.gov/tips-advice/competition-guidance/guide-antitrust-laws/dealings-competitors/price-fixing

12 Cathymcampo. (2017, December 13). Let it snow: Here's how much a great Santa can earn. Retrieved February 10, 2020, from https://www.cnbc.com/2017/12/13/santas-have-high-earning-potential-but-big-costs-too.html.

13 Leonhardt, M. (2019, December 24). Santa's pay takes a hit this year. Retrieved February 3, 2020, from https://www.cnbc.com/2019/12/23/santas-pay-takes-a-hit-this-year.html.

Ethics

14 Wenz, P. (2008). Santa Claus Oath. Retrieved April 1, 2019, from https://santaclausoath.webs.com/. This is protected ISBN # 978-0-7385-4149-5 and LCCC # 2007925452.

15 Wenz, P. (n.d.). Mrs. Claus Commission. Retrieved May 3, 2020, from https://santaclausoath.webs.com/ mrsclauscommission.htm. Used with permission from Phillip Wenz, 01 May 2020.

16 NIV. *John 13:34-35* - "A new command I give you: Love one another. As I have loved you, so you must love one another. 35 By this everyone will know that you are my disciples, if you love one another."

Special Needs Visits

17 *Autism Spectrum Disorder - A Closer Look*. (2019, February 8). Retrieved March 25, 2020, from https://www.cdc.gov/ncbddd/actearly/autism/case-modules/diagnosis/08-closer-look.html#anchor-What-are-the-core-features

18 *Autism Spectrum Disorder - A Closer Look*. (2019, February 8). Retrieved March 25, 2020, from https://www.cdc.gov/ncbddd/actearly/autism/case-modules/diagnosis/08-closer-look.html#anchor-What-are-the-core-features

19 *What is ADHD?* (2019, August 26). Retrieved March 25, 2020, from https://www.cdc.gov/ncbddd/adhd /facts.ht

20 Cerebral Palsy. (2019, March 27). Retrieved March 25, 2020, from https://www.cdc.gov/dotw/cerebral-palsy

21 *Facts about Down Syndrome.* (2019, December 5). Retrieved March 25, 2020, from https://www.cdc.gov/ncbddd/birthdefects/downsyndrome.html

22 *Health Insurance Portability and Accountability Act of 1996* (HIPAA). (2018, September 14). Retrieved March 25, 2020, from https://www.cdc.gov/phlp/publications/topic/hipaa.html

Santa Suit

23 Martin, M. (2021, December 22). Do you know the history of Santa Claus? The Oxford Eagle. Retrieved May 2, 2022, from https://www.oxfordeagle.com/2021/12/22/do-you-know-the-history-of-santa-claus/

24 NIV. *Exodus 3:5* –"Do not come any closer," God said. "Take off your sandals, for the place where you are standing is holy ground."

25 Bl. John XXIII. (1996). *Missale Romanum.* Harrison, NY: Roman Catholics Books.

26 NIV. *Ephesians 6:17* "Take the helmet of salvation and the sword of the Spirit, which is the word of God."

27 NIV. *Matthew 5:8* –"Blessed are the pure in heart, for they will see God."

28 Lawrence, J. (2013). *Priest Vestments.* Retrieved March 9, 2020, from https://www.catholicinspired.site/priest-vestments.html.

29 NKJV. *Numbers 21:8* – Then the LORD said to Moses, "Make a fiery serpent, and set it on a pole; and it shall be that everyone who is bitten, when he looks at it, shall live."

30 NIV. *Colossians 3:14* – "And over all these virtues put on love, which binds them all together in perfect unity."

31 NIV. *Galatians 5:22* – **"But the fruit of the Spirit is love, joy, peace, forbearance, kindness, goodness, faithfulness"**

32 NKJV. *Numbers 21:8* – Then the LORD said to Moses, "Make a fiery serpent, and set it on a pole; and it shall be that everyone who is bitten, when he looks at it, shall live."

33 Father W. Saunders, S. (2003). *Symbols of the Office of Bishop.* Retrieved March 9, 2020, from https://www.catholiceducation.org/en/culture/catholic-contributions/symbols-of-the-office-of-bishop.html.

34 NKJV. *Exodus 39: 27-31* – They made tunics, artistically woven of fine linen, for Aaron and his sons, 28 a turban of fine linen, exquisite hats of fine linen, short trousers of fine woven linen, 29 and a sash of fine woven linen with blue, purple, and scarlet thread, made by a weaver, as the LORD had commanded Moses. 30 Then they made the plate of the holy crown of pure gold, and wrote on it an inscription like the engraving of a signet:31 And they tied to it a blue cord, to fasten it above on the turban, as the LORD had commanded Moses.Leviticus 8:7-9 – And he put the tunic on him, girded him with the sash, clothed him with the robe, and put the ephod on him; and he girded him with the intricately woven band of the ephod, and with it tied the ephod on him. 8 Then he put the breastplate on him, and he put the Urim and the Thummim in the breastplate. 9 And he put the turban on his head. Also, on the turban, on its front, he put the golden plate, the holy crown, as the LORD had commanded Moses.

35 Father W. Saunders, S. (2003). *Symbols of the Office of Bishop.* Retrieved March 9, 2020, from https://www.catholiceducation.org/en/culture/catholic-contributions/symbols-of-the-office-of-bishop.html.

36 NKJV. *Numbers 15:38-39* – "Speak to the children of Israel: Tell them to make tassels on the corners of their garments throughout their generations, and to put a blue thread in the tassels of the corners. 39 And you shall have the tassel, that you may look upon it and remember all the commandments of the LORD and do them, and that you may not follow the harlotry to which your own heart and your own eyes are inclined."

37 Kissinger, B. (2007). *Costume Pattern.* Retrieved October 28, 2019, from https://www.stnicholascenter.org /how-to-celebrate/resources/costumes/costume-pattern.

How to Remove Odor from Your Santa Suit

38 Team, C. V. S. (2018, September 13). *7 Reasons Why You Shouldn't Use Febreze-Or Other Chemical Air Fresheners.* Retrieved February 14, 2020, from https://cvskinlabs.com/7-reasons-why-you-shouldnt-use-febreze-or-other-chemical-air-fresheners/.

Beard Care

39 Kuoppala, A. (2019, August 26). *7 Best Beard and Mustache Combs of 2019.* Retrieved February 1, 2020, from https://beardresource.com/best-beard-comb/.

40 Mouradian, w. (2018, January 16). *The Difference Between Beard Oil and Beard Balm.* Retrieved February 15, 2020, from https://www.beardbrand.com/blogs/urbanbeardsman/difference-between-beard-oil-beard-balm.

41 Sparks, H. (2019, April 15). *Men's beards carry more harmful germs than dog fur: study.* Retrieved February 15, 2020, from https://nypost.com/2019/04/15/mens-beards-carry-more-harmful-germs-than-dog-fur-study/.

Child Abuse

42 Child Welfare Information Gateway. (2019). *Mandatory Reporters of Child Abuse and Neglect.* Retrieved August 1, 2019, from https://www.childwelfare.gov/topics/systemwide/laws-policies/ statutes/manda

Beard

43 Associated Newspapers. (2019, April 13). Men with Beards Carry more Germs than Dogs with Deadly Bacteria in Their Facial Hair, Study Reveals. Daily Mail Online. Retrieved May 5, 2022, from https://www.dailymail.co.uk/news/article-6919551/Men-beards-carry-germs-DOGS-deadly-bacteria-facial-hair-study-reveals.html

Nitty Gitty

44 Bump, P. (2019, December 20). *The Breathtaking Scale of Santa Claus's Task on Christmas Eve.* Washington Post.
Retrieved September 2, 2020, from https://www.washingtonpost.com/lifestyle/2019/12/20/breathtaking-scale-santa-clauss-task-christmas-eve/

Nitty Gitty - Coal

45 *World Population Prospects - Population Division.* (n.d.). Retrieved September 02, 2020, from https://population.un.org/wpp/Download/Standard/Population/

46 Chester Energy & Policy. (2022, April 4). *Calculating Santa's coal haul for Naughty Children: An effective strategy to offset emissions? Chester Energy Policy.* Retrieved April 18, 2022, from https://www.chesterenergyandpolicy.com/blog/calculate-santa-coal-naughty-kids

Nitty Gitty - Santa Sleigh

47 Mizokami, K. (2019, December 24). *The Air Force Redesigned Santa's Sleigh for Hypersonic Speed.* Retrieved September 02, 2020, from https://www.popularmechanics.com/military/aviation/a30317765/air-force-redesign-santa-sleigh/

48 *Tracking "Big Red One": NORAD's Secret Santa Mission* [updated]. Government Book Talk. (2014, December 22). Retrieved April 18, 2022, from https://govbooktalk.gpo.gov/2014/12/22/norad-santa-tracker/

49 *Sleigh Rider One – Santa Countdown Begins!* Airservices. (2020, December 9). Retrieved April 18, 2022, from https://www.airservicesaustralia.com/santa/

Nitty Gitty - Rockfeller Center

50 Editors of Publications International, Ltd. (2007, June 26). *Christmas Trivia.* Retrieved May 13, 2020, from https://people.howstuffworks.com/culture-traditions/holidays-christmas/christmas-trivia7.htm.

Nitty Gitty - Reindeer

51 Wright, M. (2019, December 24). *USDA grants Santa Claus access to 'any border port' in the US.* Retrieved September 03, 2020, from https://www.dailymail.co.uk/news/article-7825145/USDA-grants-Santa-Claus-access-border-port-US.html

52 Foreman, M., Borrego, R., Bowman, C., Betancur, J., & Vanatta, A. (2017, February 21). *THIS JUST IN: USDA Issues Permit for Santa's Reindeer to Enter the U.S.* Retrieved September 03, 2020, from https://www.usda.gov /media/blog/2015/12/23/just-usda-issues-permit-santas-reindeer-enter-us.

Nitty Gitty - Ho Ho Ho

53 *Why Does Santa Claus Say Ho-Ho-Ho?* (n.d.). Retrieved September 15, 2020, from https://velosock.com/blogs/blog/why-does-santa-claus-say-ho-ho-ho

54 B&G Foods North America, Inc (2016) U.S. Patent No. 5,206,328. Washington, DC: U.S. Patent and Trademark Office.

55 LucasFilm Entertainment Company LTD. (1983). U.S. Patent No. 2598202. Washington, DC: U.S. Patent and Trademark Office.

Nitty Gitty - Public Domain vs Copyright

56 U.S. Copyright Office. (2020, September 4). [E-mail to the author].

70666353R00131